Automotive
ELECTRICS
A Practical Guide

Automotive
ELECTRICS
A Practical Guide

ISBN 978-0-9557418-4-5

Published by **Performance Publishing Ltd**
Unit 12, Thesiger Close, Worthing, West Sussex BN11 2RN

Author:	John Dickens
Editor:	Ian Stent
Computer Graphics:	Grapevine Print & Marketing Ltd.
Page design:	James Mansell & Richard Goodliff
Printing:	Grapevine Print & Marketing Ltd.

About the author

John Dickens was born in Leeds, Yorkshire and lived there for 20 years before obtaining a Chemistry degree at Teesside and a teaching qualification at Newcastle upon Tyne. He worked as a Chemistry teacher in the North-East of England for the next 35 years before retiring and becoming a technical writer and subsequently Technical Editor for Complete Kit Car magazine.

From an early age John was involved with motor vehicles, initially with his father's motorcycles and cars, then later with his own. He has built and owned a number of kit cars and motorcycles and also raced kit cars in the early years of the 750 MC Kit Car Challenge. John regularly contributes technical articles to a number of owners club publications and forums. He is married with two grown up sons and still lives in the Durham area.

Acknowledgements

This is my second book, and although it would have been reasonable to assume that the writing process would be easier this time around, in fact this was not the case and once again I am indebted to a number of people without whom this book would not have been completed.

Ian Stent, my editor, once again encouraged me when I was struggling for ideas or direction. Toni, my wife, not only took some of the photos that appear in the book but also managed to live with random electrical items appearing throughout the house, and put up with my constant mutterings and grumblings for longer than most people would consider reasonable.

I am also grateful to Car Builder Solutions, Stafford Vehicle Components, Premier Wiring Systems, Rapidfit Looms and Vehicle Wiring Products for kindly providing some of the samples, photographs and information which appear in this book.

Contents

Introduction

My aim, in writing this book, is to try to de-mystify the whole subject of auto-electrics. When people set out to build, customise or restore a motor vehicle they are, almost without exception, quite happy to undertake most of the mechanical aspects of a car build. They will strip, recondition and rebuild brakes, suspension and engines with hardly a second thought and yet they will almost certainly run for cover at the prospect of wiring or trimming the car themselves. A large proportion of the unfinished projects which are frequently offered for sale are described using phrases such as '90% finished, all the hard work done, just needs wiring and trim'. I am not going to pretend that wiring a car is easy, but in this book I hope to show you that it is definitely well within your capabilities.

There are a number of options open to you when the time comes to wire your car. Your choice will depend largely on how much you are prepared to do yourself and how much you are prepared to pay.

1. Have the car wired by a professional. This is the easiest option by far but also the most expensive. You will also be no nearer to understanding the wiring process and will have to rely on the professionals for future fault finding or repair.

2. Have a bespoke custom loom made for your car, or use a loom provided by your car's manufacturer, and fit it yourself. This will still be a relatively expensive process but you will save the cost of third party installation and will learn a lot more about the workings of your car's electrical system.

3. Use a 'universal' loom and fit it yourself. This will be less expensive than the previous options. At the time of writing

Using the original donor wiring loom is certainly an option, but may need minor or major modifications to fit its new environment.

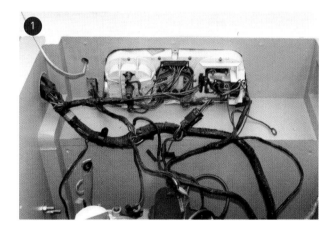

Having a wiring loom professionally made is another option.

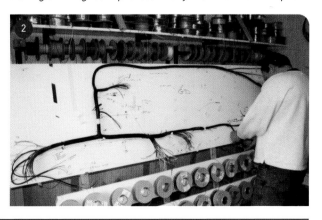

a universal loom is typically £120-£150. More work will be required in routing, trimming and fitting the loom, but the final result should be comparable with that obtained from the previous options. You will also be closer to understanding how the system works and be more able to maintain and repair it as necessary.

4. Use the complete loom from the original or donor car, modified if necessary. This will be a cheaper option still. The original loom may need to be partially stripped or dismantled to add or remove wiring and, if the modifications become extensive, you may reach the point where one of the other options becomes more sensible.

5. Produce your own custom wiring loom from scratch. This is the most labour intensive option but is also the most satisfying to complete. You will end up with your own bespoke wiring loom at a fraction of the cost of option 2 and a full working knowledge of the whole electrical system.

If you choose Option 1, then this book will still be useful to you as background information. It is my hope though that the content will also enable you to tackle any of the other options from simply connecting up a ready made loom to fabricating and fitting your own bespoke loom, wire by wire. The early chapters deal with some simple electrical theory and a closer look at the construction and operation of the various components which make up a vehicle wiring system. The later chapters deal with the practical aspects of choosing and positioning components, modifying or designing and fabricating a loom and final testing and fault finding.

You can opt for a generic new loom, designed for a front or mid-engined car.

Electricity is a form of energy just like heat, light and sound. Its existence has been recognised for a long time. Static electricity, lightning, and current electricity from biological sources were known thousands of years ago but it was not until relatively recently that people actually understood what electricity was made from. Electricity, in all its forms, is made up of electrons.

Did you pay attention in physics at school? If not it's catch up time. We believe that all materials are made up from minute particles called atoms. They are too small to be visible even with the most powerful magnifying instruments available to us. In spite of this we also believe that atoms themselves are made up from even smaller sub-atomic particles called protons, neutrons and electrons. We think an atom looks a bit like this (Fig 1).

The protons and neutrons are in the centre, called the nucleus. This is where nuclear reactions happen. The electrons orbit around the outside in layers or 'shells'. The electrons carry a negative charge (-) and the protons in the nucleus carry a positive charge (+). There is always the same amount of protons and electrons so the charges balance each other out and the atom is neutral overall.

Static electricity

If we rub some materials together hard enough, the friction between the surfaces can drag some of the electrons from one surface onto the other. The surface which collects the extra electrons ends up with a negative charge and the surface which loses the electrons ends up with an unbalanced positive charge (Fig 2). If the materials are conductors, the charge instantly flows away but if the materials do not conduct electricity, the charges remain

This is a simplified idea of what we think an atom looks like.

The friction causes electrons to rub off the plastic surface and onto the cloth.

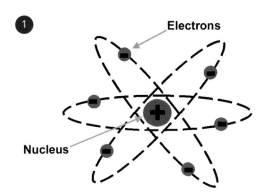

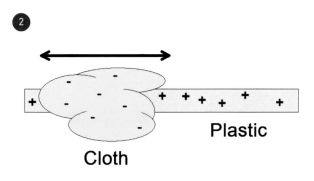

on the surface for some time. These are static electric charges.

This effect is what makes your hair stick to a plastic comb after use, or enables you to stick a balloon to the wall after rubbing it on a woollen jumper. Static electricity has many uses in industry, such as powder-coating, and waste gas purification, but in the automotive world it has mostly nuisance value. It is the reason why you get a shock from the car door handle after sliding across the cloth seat to get out. It is also the reason why F1 cars used to drive over earthing straps as they stop at their pit to re-fuel. The friction of the air as they move at high speed can cause a static charge to build up on the outer surface of the car. This charge can cause a spark to jump from the car to the fuel rig as it is connected, with potentially disastrous consequences. Aircraft fires have been caused in this way.

Current electricity

In some materials, particularly metals, the outermost electrons on the atoms are not held particularly tightly and are free to move randomly between adjacent atoms. If we connect a power source to these materials, all the electrons move from atom to atom in the same direction and form an electric current (Fig 3).

Materials with lots of free electrons will allow an electric current to flow through them easily. They are called conductors. Silver is the best conductor but is far too expensive for general wiring use. Copper is the best alternative, closely followed by aluminium.

Materials with very few or no free electrons will not allow electricity to flow through them at all. They are known as insulators (or non-conductors). Glass, plastics and ceramics are all commonly used as insulators.

In between these two extremes are materials which allow electricity to flow in a restricted fashion. They are called resistors. Carbon, in its graphite form, and an alloy called nichrome are materials commonly used to produce resistors.

A power source, such as a battery, produces a force which pushes the electrons through the conductor. This is called the Electro-Motive Force (emf) and is measured in Volts (V). Very few people use the term emf and it is commonly just referred to as the voltage.

The actual amount of electricity flowing through a conductor is called the current and is measured in amperes or amps (A). High currents flowing through materials can cause them to heat up quickly, especially materials which resist the current flow. The degree to which a material restricts the flow of electricity is called its resistance and this is measured in Ohms (Ω).

These three properties are related to each other. If we increase the resistance in a circuit, the current flowing round it will be reduced. We can restore the current again by increasing the voltage to force more electrons around the circuit. Not surprisingly there is a formula for this. (This is physics after all). It is called Ohms Law.

The power source causes electrons to move from atom to atom to form a flow of electric current.

It is commonly written as...

$$V = IR$$

Which translates as...

Voltage = Current x Resistance

We can shuffle this formula around to use it to work out current or resistance too.

Current = Voltage / Resistance

And...

Resistance = Voltage / Current

There is a fourth term that we commonly use in electrical work and that is power. The power of an electrical component is measured in Watts (W) or kilowatts (kW).

It won't surprise you to know that the power is also related to the quantity of electricity flowing in a circuit and that there is a formula for this too.

Power = Voltage x Current

And if we shuffle this formula too we get...

Voltage = Power / Current

And...

Current = Power / Voltage

This last version is particularly useful for working out how much current a component will draw. We need to know this in order to choose a suitable value for a fuse. If, for example, we want a suitable fuse for a pair of 60W halogen headlights we simply put the numbers into the formula. Two 60W lights will have a total power of 120W and the nominal voltage of a car system is 12V.

Current = 120w / 12v
Current = 10A

The formula tells us that the lights will draw a current of 10 amps. We don't want the fuse to blow in normal use so we need some headroom to allow for surges when the lights are switched on and off. In this example a suitable fuse for the circuit would be around 15A.

Electrical circuits

An electric current will not flow unless there is a power source and a complete circuit of conducting material. If the circuit is interrupted at any point the current stops.

A basic electrical circuit would look like this (Fig 4). The bulb lights as the circuit is complete. The wires and bulb are all conductors. The bulb does have some resistance but not enough to prevent current flow.

So which way does the current actually flow? Well there are two types of electric current. Your domestic electricity supply is 230v AC, 50 Hz. The voltage is 230v but the AC designation means that the supply has an alternating current. The direction of the current flow reverses rapidly and constantly. In fact it reverses 50 times every second. This is what the 50 Hz means. AC is fine for lighting and heating but you cannot charge a battery or power an ignition system with AC. Systems which are dependent on batteries use DC. The term DC means direct current. It constantly flows in the same direction, but deciding which direction caused us a problem in the past. Years before we knew what electricity actually was, it became

This simple circuit will light the bulb but there is no way to turn it off.

4

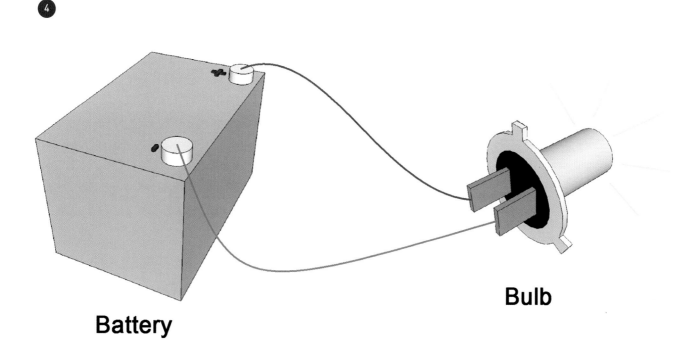

Battery

Bulb

necessary, for various reasons, to decide which direction it travelled. It was decided (wrongly as it turned out) that the direction of flow was from the positive terminal to the negative. This is called Conventional Current. When we discovered that electricity was made up from negatively charged electrons we realised that it actually flows from the negative terminal to the positive. This is known as Actual Current. Rather than re-write all the text books and scientific papers, it was decided to stick with the conventional idea of current flow. For our purposes it really makes no difference either way.

Although the simple circuit shown in figure 4 will light the bulb perfectly well, it would be totally useless in practice since the only way of turning the bulb off is to cut or disconnect one of the wires. We need some convenient means of interrupting and re-establishing the circuit. This, of course, is a switch.

Using this circuit (Fig 5) we can switch the bulb on and off as required. If we were going to use this circuit in a car it would also be advisable to add a fuse to the circuit as a safety device in case of faulty wiring or components.

If wires become chaffed or disconnected it is possible to get a condition known as a short circuit or 'short'. In figure 6 one of the wires supplying power to the bulb has become disconnected and is touching the other terminal.

The bulb will stop working as current is no longer flowing through it. There is a more serious problem though. We have

a short circuit. With the bulb bypassed, there is no resistance in the circuit so a high current will flow through the wires. They will heat up rapidly and may melt or set fire to the insulation or harness. A fuse, wired as shown in figure 7 will protect the circuit. A fuse is simply a piece of thin wire which gets hot and melts if too much current passes through it. This effectively switches off the electricity supply before damage can occur to the rest of the wiring or components. By using different wire thicknesses, fuses of different ratings can be produced.

We normally place the fuse in the circuit before any other component so that more of the circuit is protected.

Series and parallel circuits

More bad memories from school? I promise we're getting near the end now.

Many circuits on a car have more than one component in them. The sidelight circuit, for example, contains the battery, a fuse, the light switch, two rear light bulbs, two sidelight bulbs, a number plate light bulb and all the instrument lighting bulbs. Multiple components can be interconnected in one of two basic ways.

1. In series

The three bulbs here are connected in series (Fig 8). All the electricity passes through each bulb in turn. This is how the

This circuit allows us to turn the bulb on or off as needed.

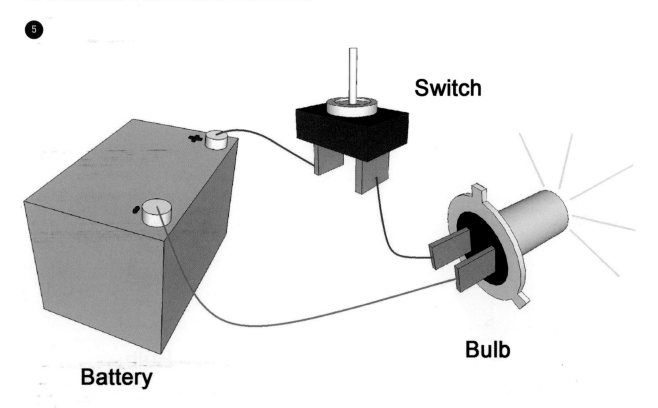

5

Switch

Bulb

Battery

A wire has become disconnected and is touching the other bulb terminal.

6

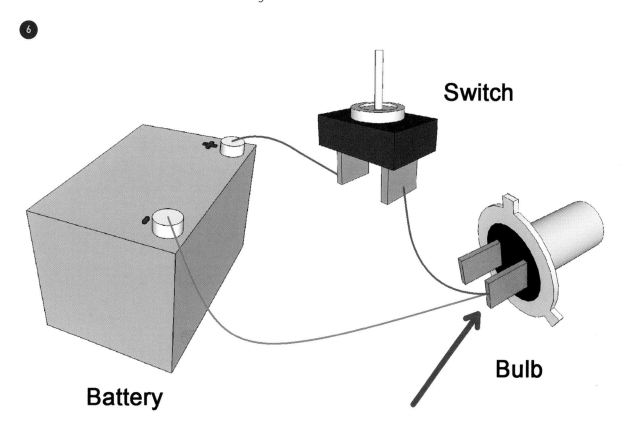

Switch

Battery

Bulb

This circuit is protected against faults by the fuse. It will 'blow' if too much current flows

7

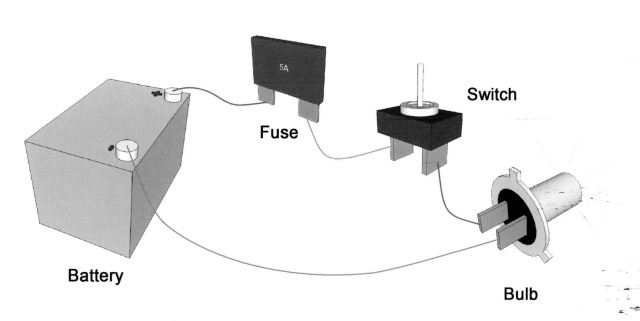

5A

Fuse

Switch

Battery

Bulb

old Christmas tree lights were connected and they have the same drawback too. A blown bulb or a break in the circuit will stop all the bulbs from working. Car lighting circuits are not connected like this.

2. In parallel

The three bulbs here (Fig 9) are connected in parallel. Each bulb effectively has its own circuit so a blown bulb or a fault in one circuit will not affect the others and they will continue to work. House lights and car lights are connected like this.

In practice most circuits are a combination of these two systems. Switches and fuses need to control all the components in a circuit, so we would wire them in series but multiple components like lights would be wired in parallel within the circuit.

Circuit diagrams

The use of graphics to illustrate the circuits in the previous examples is nice for clarity but becomes less practical as circuits become more complex. Instead there is an internationally agreed set of circuit symbols which are normally used to draw circuit diagrams. You do not have to use them when you draw your own circuits but you need to understand them if you are looking at circuits drawn by other people. They are generally very simplified for ease of drawing (Fig 10–15).

These are all general electrical symbols. There are other more specific ones for auto-electrical components.

Using these symbols greatly simplifies the job of drawing out a circuit. If we draw the circuit shown in figure 7 using these symbols it would look like this (Fig 16).

Earths

In figure 11 there is a symbol labelled as Earth. In automotive electrical systems this is a device used to simplify the wiring. We know that electricity will not flow unless there is a complete circuit so we not only need wires carrying the current from the battery to the component but, in order to complete the circuit, we need wires carrying the current back again. Car manufacturers take advantage of the fact that their vehicles are constructed largely from steel and use the steel bodywork as the return path for the electric current. The body of the car is called the earth.

Since around 1950 all vehicles have been wired with a negative earth. This means that the negative terminal of the battery is connected to the steel structure of the vehicle, normally by a heavy duty cable or braided strap. The amount of wiring used can then be greatly reduced as there is no need for each circuit to have a wire carrying the current back to the battery. If we bolt a horn, for example, to the steel bodywork of a car only a power supply is needed as the battery and horn are both already connected to earth (Fig 17).

At the time of writing, there are developments in vehicle wiring which threaten to make much of this chapter redundant, although for restorers and customisers I suspect this will take quite some time yet. As vehicles have become more complex the amount and weight of the wiring required

In series. All the bulbs are effectively in the same circuit. If one fails they all stop working.

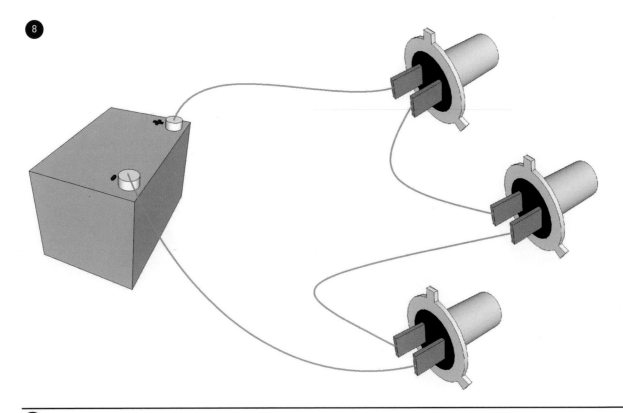

8

In parallel. Each bulb is independent of the rest and will continue to work if one, or both, of the others fails.

9

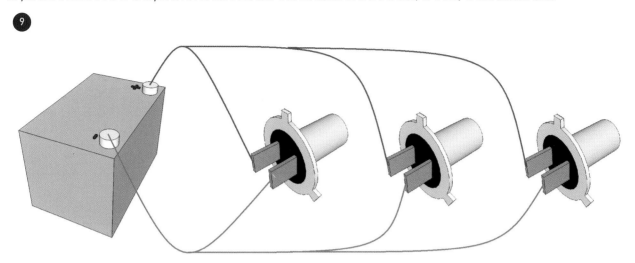

has become a significant factor in its design, development and manufacturing costs. In order to reduce the wiring, manufacturers have introduced multiplexing systems. Bosch designed a system in which a number of ECUs or processors are mounted around the vehicle to control all its electrical

functions. They are connected by only one or two wires known as a 'data bus'.

Coded data is passed around the system and each ECU checks the data to see if needs to take any action or ignore it. When required the ECUs switch on the various electrical

Wires are represented by simple straight lines, although in practice their routing or shape makes no difference whatsoever.

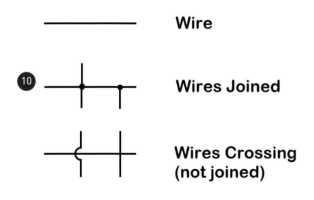

Wire

10 **Wires Joined**

Wires Crossing (not joined)

A lighting lamp is a bulb providing illumination, for example a headlight. In a car an indicator lamp is normally something like the ignition warning light.

12 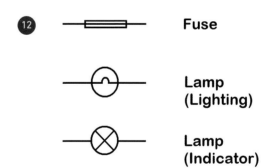 **Fuse**

Lamp (Lighting)

Lamp (Indicator)

A cell is a single unit. A battery is a collection of linked cells. A car battery has six 2v cells connected in series to produce 12v.

11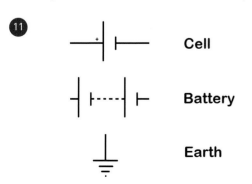

Cell

Battery

Earth

An ammeter used to be a common fitment in a car but since alternators replaced dynamos in the charging system a voltmeter or battery condition meter is more usual.

13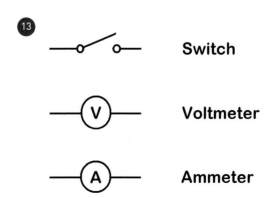

Switch

Voltmeter

Ammeter

components. Examples of multiplexing systems are CAN (Controlled Area Network), LIN (Local Interconnect Network) and MOST (Media Oriented System Transport). The last system was designed for the much faster data transfer rates needed for DVD, TV and stereo sound signals and uses fibre optics rather than copper wiring to carry the signals.

Hopefully I will never have to deal with any of these systems on a level deeper than bewildered owner, and it is certainly not my intention to discuss them in more detail in this book.

In this chapter I have tried to explain, in simple terms, how electricity works. Don't be too concerned about the theories and formulae here. You may need them occasionally but you can certainly rewire a car without doing any hard sums at all. The following chapters will be far more concerned with the individual components and systems and the practical aspects of wiring up a motor vehicle.

Variable resistors would be used in cars to vary the heater fan speed or to dim the instrument panel lights.

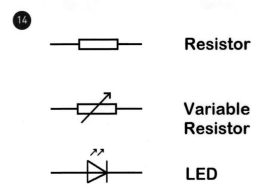

This circuit could be read by any electrical engineer whereas Figure 7 uses my own symbols which are certainly not universally understood.

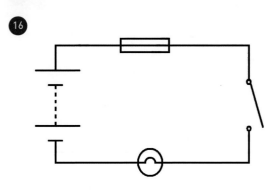

These are the more specialised symbols that are used in auto electrical circuits.

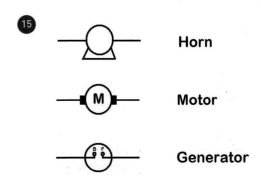

This circuit is completed by the fact that both the battery and the horn are connected to earth (the car bodywork).

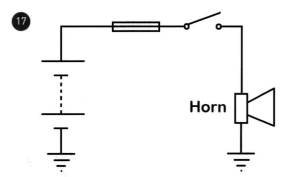

02 Power Supplies

Dynamos, alternators, batteries and fuses

Generator

The engine driven generator of a car is its primary power source. The battery is simply there to start the car. Once the engine is running, the generator powers all the electrical components and also provides the current needed to recharge the battery ready for the next start-up.

Michael Faraday was the first person to establish the link between electricity and magnetism. He found that when a magnet was moved in a coil of wire, an electric current was produced (Fig 1).

The direction of the electric current depended on the direction of movement or which pole of the magnet was being used (Fig 2).

The size of the voltage depends on the strength of the magnet, the speed of movement and the number of turns of wire in the coil.

In a basic generator it is easier to spin the coil of wire and keep the magnet still (Fig 3).

The problem with this simple generator was that every time one section of the coil moved from the North to the South Pole, the electric current reversed direction. It produced alternating current (AC) (Fig 4).

To charge a vehicle battery direct current (DC) was needed, so the coil output was modified using a split commutator and carbon brushes to switch the coil connections as it rotated. This resulted in a workable dynamo (Fig 5).

A simple dynamo like this will produce a series of pulses rather than a smooth DC current (Fig 6).

A smoother output can be obtained by using multiple coils of wire, each with its own pair of commutator segments (Fig 7).

The greater the number of coils used, the smoother the

A magnet moving in a coil will produce an electric current. The current only flows when the magnet is actually moving.

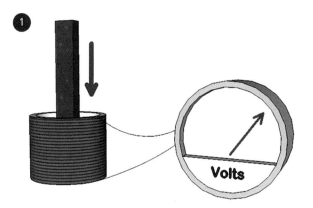

If the magnet is moved in the opposite direction the electric current also reverses its direction of flow.

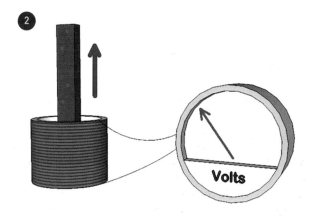

A simple coil spinning in a magnetic field will produce a series of alternating current pulses.

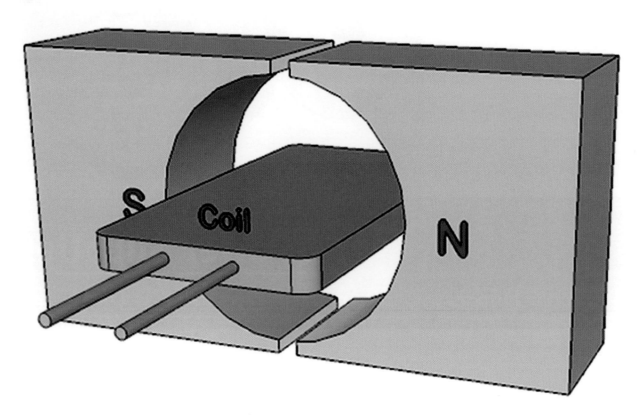

A single coil spinning in a magnetic field produces a series of current pulses which reverse direction as it spins (AC).

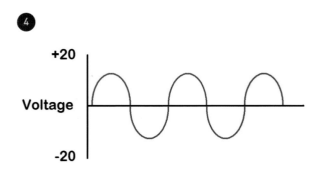

resulting output current will be (Fig 8).

The output of a dynamo is normally regulated by an electromechanical control box which alters the strength of the magnetic field to control the voltage generated by the dynamo.

The bulky coils and the commutator limit the maximum speed at which a dynamo can be rotated. If the dynamo is geared so that it does not over rev when the engine is turning at its maximum speed, it will not be spinning fast enough to charge the vehicle battery when the car engine is idling. It was quite common for the ignition warning light to be

glowing at idle on a dynamo equipped vehicle. In fact this was sometimes used to adjust the idle speed on these engines.

As electrical equipment became more power hungry with the use of heated rear windows etc. the dynamo was no longer able to cope. Fortunately help was at hand in the form of the far more efficient alternator. In the '60s semiconductor technology was sufficiently advanced to be able to produce reliable solid state rectifiers which could convert the AC output from an alternator into the DC needed to charge the battery. Semiconductors were also used to manufacture control units able to regulate the output voltage to a suitable level. An alternator uses a lighter more compact rotating magnet with continuous slip rings rather than a split commutator, so it can be spun much faster than a dynamo (Fig 9).

As a result, alternators have a much higher output than dynamos and will charge the battery even when the engine is idling. With the much greater demands of modern auto electrical systems, all modern cars use an alternator based charging system.

Alternator ratings

Alternators are normally rated by their maximum output current (in amps). The Lucas ACR series of alternators for example, as fitted to British cars in the '70s and '80s, were generally physically interchangeable and available with various outputs.

ACR 15	27 amps
ACR 16	34 amps
ACR 17	38 amps
ACR 18	43 amps

Most owners are quite happy to use the alternator already fitted to the engine as standard, but if you need to fit a different unit due to space considerations or if you wish to fit a smaller and lighter competition unit, you need to know that its output will be sufficient to meet your needs. Fitting an alternator with too low an output will mean that under high load conditions the battery will be making up the shortfall and will slowly lose its charge. There are no serious problems in fitting an alternator with a higher output than necessary, but it will need more engine power to drive it, with obvious consequences for fuel consumption and emissions.

Battery

Lead acid batteries have been with us for around 150 years now. They are big and heavy and contain corrosive sulphuric acid. The lead content is also toxic, so proper disposal of spent batteries is essential. In spite of these drawbacks they are still the first choice for vehicle applications because they are robust and reliable and because of their low cost.

Construction – The plates in a battery are grids made from lead alloy containing spongy metallic lead paste in the cathode (negative) and lead-dioxide paste in the anode (positive) (Fig 10).

To increase the surface area, and therefore the battery capacity, each cell contains a number of thin plates in an electrolyte of sulphuric acid solution (Fig 11).

The voltage produced by a single cell is 2.1 Volts. To produce a 12v battery (actually 12.6v) six individual cells are linked together in series (Fig 12).

A single coil with a split commutator will produce a series of direct current pulses.

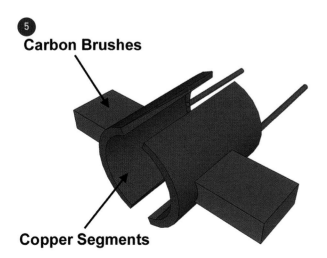

5

Carbon Brushes

Copper Segments

Battery types – Pure lead is too soft to produce strong thin grids, so originally antimony was alloyed with the lead to improve its strength. Unfortunately the antimony in the grid alloy caused greater water loss when charging (gassing) and faster self discharge in storage. Different alloys have been developed to overcome this.

Low maintenance batteries use calcium or selenium

The dynamo produces direct current, but if only one coil is used the current is a series of individual pulses.

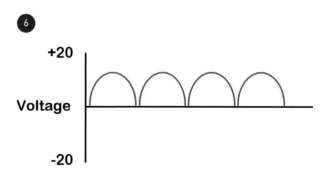

6

If a number of coils are used, the current pulses overlap to become a steady flow of DC current.

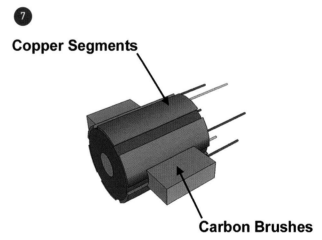

7

Copper Segments

Carbon Brushes

The pulses of current from the individual coils start to overlap and produce a constant output current.

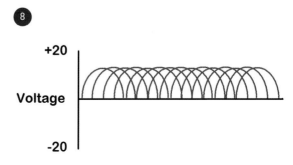

8

As simple as it gets. A motorcycle alternator showing the stationary coils and the rotating permanent magnet. The regulator in this case is a separate unit.

The positive and negative battery plates are both lead alloy grids but contain different chemicals within the grids.

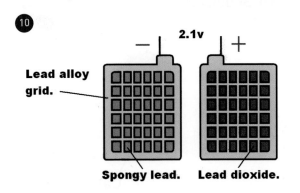

A single cell contains a number of positive and negative plates and produces 2.1v.

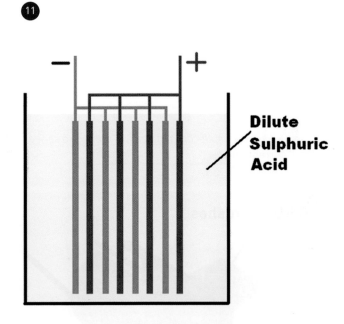

alloyed with the lead. These provide the mechanical strength, but reduce water loss and self-discharge. More recently silver has also been added to the calcium-lead alloy making it extremely temperature stable and corrosion resistant, significantly lengthening battery life.

Sealed batteries were introduced once gassing had been minimised. The latest types are actually Valve Regulated Lead Acid (VRLA) where the battery is fully sealed to prevent water loss and contains a catalyst to recombine any hydrogen and oxygen produced but is vented by a valve if excess pressure does build up.

More recent improvements have concentrated on the sulphuric acid electrolyte. By immobilising the electrolyte, spillage has been prevented giving greater freedom in mounting the battery.

Gel batteries have silica added to the acid to turn it to a semi solid gel, making them spill proof. They are also more suitable for deep discharge than standard batteries but are very sensitive to overcharging. They must be charged at a lower voltage and therefore may need a special charger.

A car battery contains six individual cells connected in series to produce an output of 12.6v.

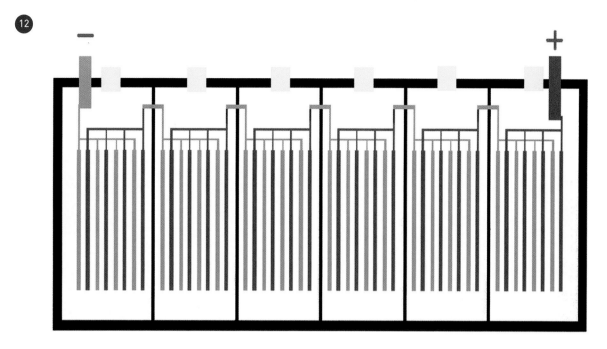

A typical automatic battery charger. It can be left connected to the battery for long periods of time and will maintain it in peak condition

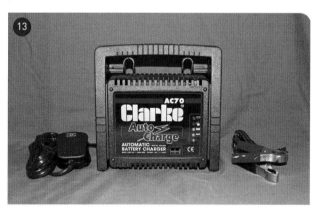

A basic fuse box similar to that used in a classic Mini.

A modern car fuse box showing the bewildering array of fuses

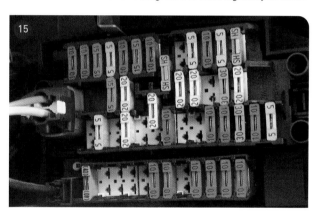

Glass bodied cartridge fuses. These are very similar to household fuses. The internal wire is visible so that it can be checked once the fuse is removed.

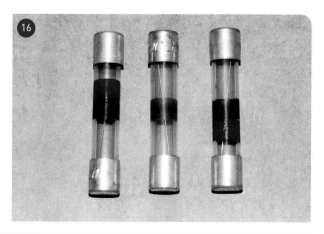

These 'Continental' type fuses originally had ceramic bodies like the three on the left. The yellow 5A fuse has a plastic body. Once again the conductor is visible for checking.

Blade fuses are commonly used in modern cars. They are compact and have a very positive location in their fitting giving trouble free connections.

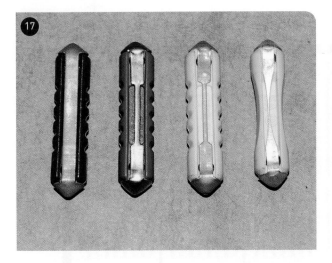

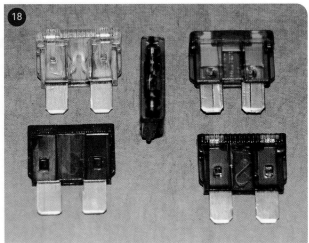

Check suitability before you buy a charger for a gel battery.

Absorbed Glass Mat (AGM) batteries have a liquid electrolyte but it is absorbed into glassfibre matting between the plates, so there is no free liquid. The battery can be mounted on its side or even upside down. No liquid will spill even if the casing is cracked. The plates are often spiral wound to increase their surface area and capacity even further.

AGM batteries can produce higher currents and can be discharged more deeply. They also have very low self discharge rates, typically losing only 1–3 per cent of their charge per month, so they are more suitable for cars used less frequently.

Battery capacity – One way of rating batteries is by their capacity in amp hours. The measurement is taken over a 20 hour discharge time, so a battery rated at 45 amp hours will supply a continuous current of 2.25 amps for 20 hours. A 60 amp hour battery will supply a continuous current of 3 amps for 20 hours. An alternative rating system is the cold cranking current. This is measured at -18deg C and is the current the battery can deliver for a specified time before the voltage drops to a specified end voltage. There are three standards. BS, DIN and SAE. The SAE rating is measured over 30 seconds and the end voltage is 7.2v. The final battery rating system is Reserve Capacity. A constant current of 25A is drawn from the battery and the time taken for the output voltage to fall to 10.5v is measured. This test is carried out at 25deg C.

Battery care – Modern batteries are very reliable if treated correctly, but there are still a couple of points to watch.

Impacts can crack the casing or damage the internal structure. Vibration can also dislodge material from the plates. Sensible handling and mounting will prevent this.

Batteries are not designed to be regularly discharged below 50 per cent capacity and can fail after as few as 50

deep cycles. In automotive use this should not be a problem as the battery is usually quickly recharged after use.

For cars used infrequently or laid up over winter, sulphation is the main danger. Sulphation is the formation of permanent lead sulphate crystals on the plates causing partial or total failure. It happens when a battery is left discharged or with a low electrolyte level for long periods. A lead/antimony battery can lose 2–10 per cent of its charge per week, so to avoid sulphation in storage regular charging is needed. On the other hand, overcharging can distort the plates and cause water loss. A simple trickle charger may be adequate but the best solution is to use one of the newer computer controlled battery chargers or 'conditioners'. They are designed to be permanently connected to the battery and have a multi stage charging and maintenance cycle (Fig 13).

Fuse box

This is the main power take off point for almost every system on the car. Ignition circuits were commonly left un-fused but modern ECUs incorporating delicate microprocessors now need fused power supplies too. Since the fuse is the principal safety feature in a circuit it is not surprising that the number of fuses used in motor vehicles has increased dramatically in recent years.

The original Minis used two fuses for the whole car (Fig 14).

Modern cars use a great many more (Fig 15). Almost every single component has its own fuse and a 'map' is needed to identify the individual functions when a fault does occur.

The construction of the actual fuses has changed too. Originally cartridge fuses similar to those used in 13A plugs were used in the UK (Fig 16) with porcelain 'bullet' type fuses being favoured on the continent (Fig 17).

Blade type fuses are the most common now. They are

compact, locate positively and are easy to check without removing them from their location (Fig 18).

There are now some interesting alternatives available to use in place of standard blade fuses. Replacements are available with a built in light. In normal use the current bypasses the light and flows directly through the fuse, but if the fuse blows the light then illuminates to show which fuse is damaged. It is also possible to obtain miniature circuit breakers which fit into the same location as a blade fuse but can be reset rather than replaced if a fault causes them to open.

Some cars incorporate a 'fusible link' in some circuits. This is basically a wire which is designed to behave like a fuse in the event of an overload. These links are not always easy to spot as they look very similar to a normal wire. They are generally a little larger in diameter and have different fireproof insulation. A better alternative to the fusible link is the Strip Fuse, the Midi Fuse or the Mega Fuse.

Fuses of this type are used in the main power circuits of a car, often mounted directly to the battery. In this way they will protect the entire electrical system from a catastrophic failure.

Once the power has been produced by the generator, stored in the battery or distributed by the fuse box it has to be carried around the car to where it is needed. The next chapter looks, in detail, at the way this is achieved.

03 Carrying The Current
Wires, connectors and earths

Wires

As we have seen, electricity will only flow around a complete circuit of conducting material. In a car most of the conducting material will be either copper in the form of wires or steel in the form of the car body earth return. Copper is used since, apart from silver, it is the best metallic conductor. As with all metals though, the conductivity of copper is reduced by the presence of impurities. Copper used in electrical wiring must be 99.99% pure or better. For a given wire diameter the best conductor will be one with a single solid copper core just like those used in house wiring systems. Unfortunately this is not practical for most other applications. Even though copper is one of the most malleable metals, a single solid core, if subjected to repeated movement or bending, would fatigue and break very quickly. To avoid this, all electrical wiring in common use is made up of a number of fine strands of copper surrounded by a flexible insulating material, normally PVC (Fig 1).

The size and number of copper strands in a wire will determine how much current the wire can safely carry without overheating (Fig 2). A typical wire specification would look like this:

16/0.20mm, 0.5mm^2

The first number tells us how many strands of wire are used. In this example 16 strands are used.

The second number tells us the diameter of each individual strand. In this case each strand

is 0.2mm diameter. Common sizes are 0.2 and 0.3mm.

The third number tells us the total cross sectional area of the wire. This particular wire has a total area of 0.5mm^2.

The insulating material can affect the capability of the wire too. Modern automotive wiring is of the 'thinwall' type which has an outer insulation made from a thinner layer of a harder grade of PVC. This allows the wire to carry a higher current safely. It also gives the wire a smaller overall diameter and a lower weight (Fig 3). This means that a completed harness of thinwall wire will be smaller and lighter that one made from conventional wire. This may be

A typical PVC insulated wire with 13 strands of 0.3mm diameter copper wire.

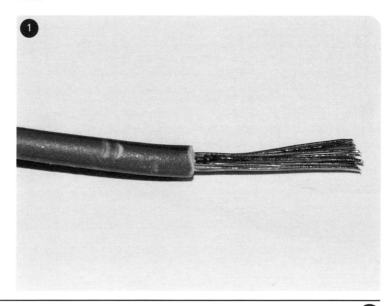

significant in a competition car or where a very complex loom is needed.

As a guide, here are some common wiring dimensions with their safe continuous current ratings.

16/0.20mm	0.5mm²	11.0A
32/0.20mm	1.0mm²	16.5A
28/0.3mm	2.0mm²	25.0A
44/0.3mm	3.0mm²	33.0A
56/0.3mm	4.0mm²	39.0A
84/0.3mm	6.0mm²	50.0A

Battery and starter motor cables have to carry a very high current, so a typical battery cable would have a specification something like this.

37/0.90mm	25mm²	170A

This would be a semi-rigid cable as it has a relatively small number of thick strands. Flexible battery cable or welding cable, which is sometimes used, has a larger number of fine strands (Fig 4). For example...

194/0.40mm	25mm²	170A

Selecting the correct wire type

If you want to buy some wire to replace, repair or modify an existing loom, you need to know how much current it will be

A 32/0.20mm wire alongside a 56/0.3mm wire. The thinner wire can safely carry 16A, the thicker wire close to 40A.

A standard wire (top) and its thinwall equivalent (bottom). The difference is not huge in a single wire but in a loom containing 20 or more wires it becomes very significant.

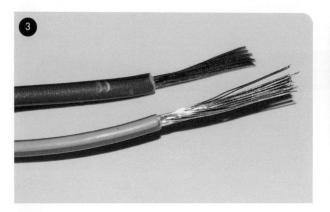

expected to carry. You can do this using the formula I gave you in Chapter 1.

$$Amps = Watts/Volts$$

As an example we will work out what is needed to wire a set of indicators fitted with the commonly used 12v - 21w bulbs.

Putting the numbers in the formula we get...

$$Amps = 21/12$$
$$Amps = 1.75A$$

So each bulb will only draw a current of 1.75A. In normal use, though, there will always be two indicator bulbs on at the same time, so the supply side of the circuit will have to provide 3.5A (2x1.75A). If we want to use the same circuit for the hazard warning lights too, then we must be aware that all four bulbs will flash together, so we then need to supply 7A (4x1.75A). This is not a problem since even the smallest wire size in common use, the 16/0.20mm, will carry 11A safely. If you wanted to build in a bigger safety margin still, you could use the next size up, the 32/0.20mm, which will safely carry 16.6A. Don't forget that any earth return wiring that you use must also be capable of carrying the same current. If you have a GRP car you may choose to earth a number of circuits to a common point. If you do this then remember that the main earth return back to the battery must be capable of carrying the total current used by all the circuits earthed to it.

Don't try to cut costs on battery and starter cables, especially if you mount the battery and starter motor at opposite ends of the car. Smaller diameter (read cheaper) cables will heat up as they carry the huge current needed to start the car. Heat causes the resistance of the wire to increase and over a longer length of wire this can significantly reduce the current reaching the starter motor. Use larger diameter cables with a high current rating for both the power supply and the earth return.

In fact, this is good advice for the whole of the car wiring. It is a time consuming job that you really only want to do once, so always use good quality wiring with plenty of current carrying capacity.

Flexible battery cable made up of almost 200 separate 0.4mm strands.

Connectors

The purpose of a connector in an electrical circuit is to enable a component or a section of the loom to be quickly and conveniently disconnected and reconnected for removal and replacement, without having to re-solder or re-crimp the wiring. Over the years, manufacturers have used a bewildering array of electrical connectors and terminals in their cars and, in fact, still continue to do so. Despite some attempts at standardisation it is rare to find matching plugs and connectors used on cars manufactured in different countries or continents. This lack of standardisation makes it difficult for us, as home builders, to obtain small quantities or individual examples of plugs or sockets which will mate up with those found on production car looms. On the up side, there is a wider range of connectors available to us now than there has ever been and this enables us to produce our own wiring which is at least up to production standards, if not better.

Types of connectors

The first choice you need to make is whether you intend to solder or crimp the connections. Soldering can produce

These spade or Lucar terminals have separate insulating sleeves and can be soldered or crimped onto the wires.

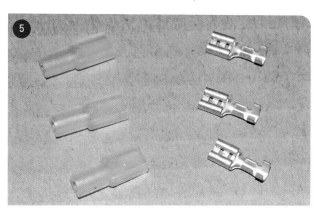

Pre-insulated crimp connectors. The red colour coding shows that they are suitable for smaller wires with a cross section of 0.65 - 1.50 mm².

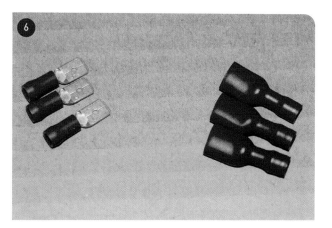

These are male and female bullet connectors for the same small diameter wires.

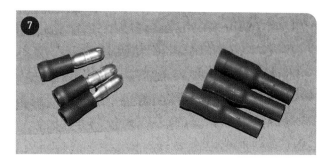

Although these bullet connectors look similar to the ones in Fig 7 they will not interconnect. They are for larger wires with areas of 1.5 – 2.5 mm².

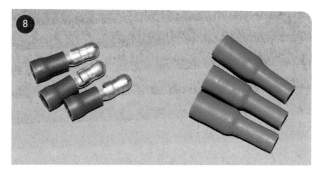

A variety of different sized loop connectors. They are normally used to connect earth wires to screws or bolts.

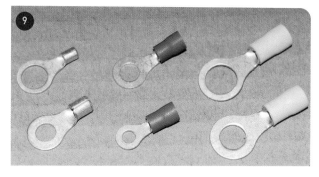

This is a Scotchlok type connector. It is designed to 'tap' into an existing wire to connect another lead to it. Personally I do not like these as they cut through the existing insulation to make the connection.

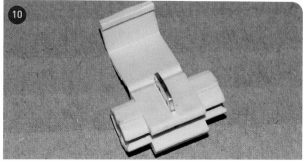

The battery terminal clamps (left) can be attached to the cables by screw fittings. The terminals supplied with the battery master switch (right) need to be crimped or soldered.

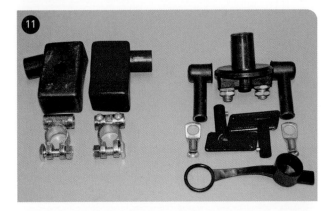

Battery or earth strap terminals need to carry a high current. I prefer to solder them but a special crimping tool is available

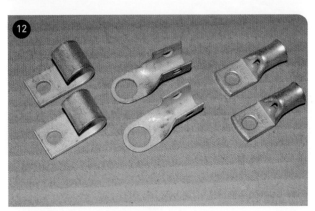

excellent low resistance connections but must be done carefully to avoid problems. The finished connection needs support to avoid movement, as the solder can cause the wire to become brittle and it will snap if allowed to flex. You may wish to solder only the terminals which will carry a high current such as alternator wires, main feeds to light and ignition switches and the heavy duty battery and starter motor cables.

There are advantages and disadvantages to both soldered and crimped connections, however nowadays almost all professionally produced looms, and especially those used in aerospace applications, use exclusively crimped terminals. Good crimped connections are certainly quicker and easier to produce than good soldered connections, and the tools required are cheaper too. There is a wide range of pre-insulated and non-insulated terminals available (Fig 5-9). At the moment the most commonly used type seems to be the pre-insulated terminals. It is also possible to get terminals with heat shrink tubing already attached, so that the connection can be sealed once it has been crimped.

If you need to 'tap' or connect into an existing wire or loom, the correct method is to strip off some insulation, solder in the new wire, then re-insulate the joint, but this is tricky so a quick alternative is to use a 'Scotchlock' (Fig 10). Personally I do not use these as they cut through the insulation and expose the bare wire to the elements.

Battery and earth connections need to carry a very high current and they tend to be very specialised (Fig 11/12). Special crimping tools are available should you wish to use them, but for high current applications I tend to prefer to solder the connectors into place.

Multiplugs can be very useful if you need to produce a wiring loom in sections or if you intend to have quickly detachable body panels, such as a removable front end or

2, 4, 6 and 8-way multiplugs which use standard 6mm blade connectors

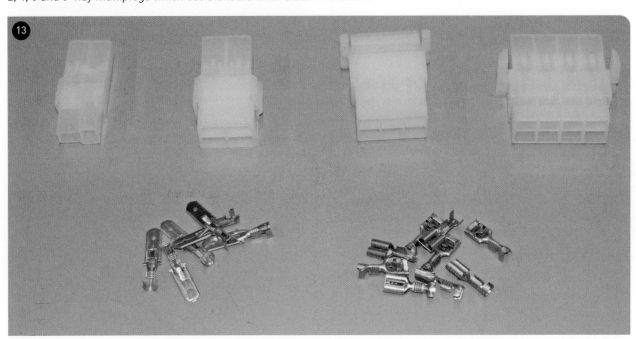

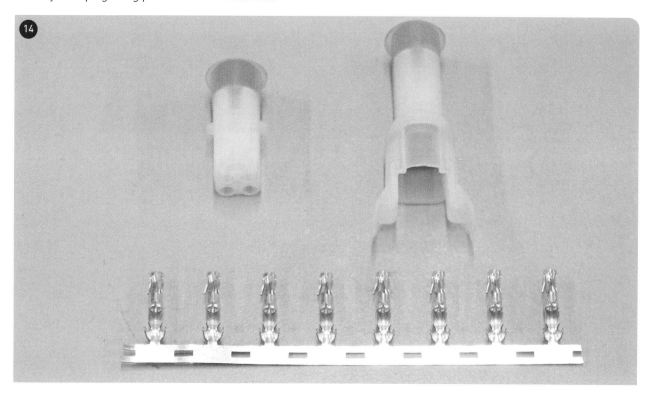

rear clam. They are also quicker to use and look a lot neater than a collection of individual spade or bullet connectors.

Some multiplugs are simply plastic receptacles which can hold and locate standard male and female blade connectors (Fig 13).

If the connector is likely to be exposed to the elements it is worth spending a little more on fully waterproof multiplugs (Fig 15). The small price premium will pay off in the future.

There are also some specialised multiplugs which are needed for specific electrical components (Fig 16).

Connectors must always be free from dirt or corrosion and must fit together firmly. Even brand new connectors have a very small resistance between the two sections and this can cause a drop in voltage across the joint. A typical large connector, when new, will have a voltage drop of 10 millivolts (0.01v) per amp of current flowing. In a car headlamp circuit flowing 10 amps this would give a voltage drop of 0.1v across each connector. Over the whole length of the light circuit there could easily be five separate connections, so a total voltage drop of 0.5v is certainly possible. Once the connectors start to corrode or become dirty, the voltage drop will increase dramatically and in extreme cases the connection can fail completely.

Earths

As discussed in Chapter 1, production car manufacturers cut down on the amount of wiring needed by using the metal car body to provide the return path for the electric current once it has passed through the various components. The saving in time and materials is significant for a major

manufacturer, but the system has its drawbacks too. Steel is not the best conductor and, in fact, has a significant electrical resistance but this is more than offset by the large amount of steel available for the current to flow through. The more significant problem with steel is that of corrosion. In order to obtain an electrical contact, any paint or other coating has to be removed from the steel at all the earthing points. The bare metal corrodes and the electrical resistance of the junction increases as the rust slowly separates the wiring and the bodywork, causing a poor and eventually non-existent connection. These 'bad earths' are a common cause of electrical problems as cars age. In

A waterproof 5-way multiplug using pin connectors.

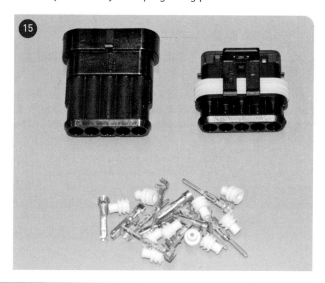

Clockwise from the top left are a twin filament headlamp bulb connector, a Lucas alternator plug and an instrument light bulb holder.

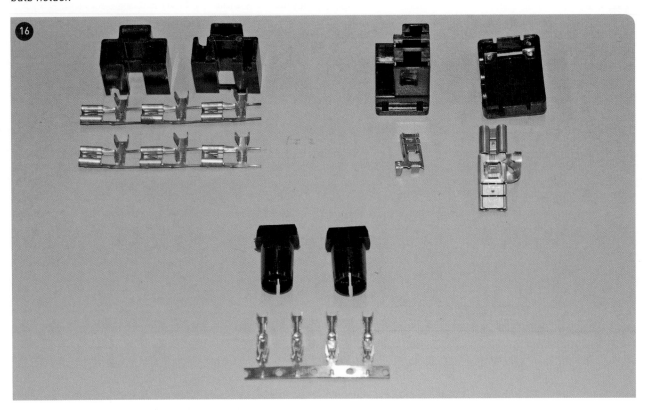

A braided wire earthing strap connecting a galvanised steel subframe directly to the negative battery terminal.

addition, components such as the engine and gearbox, which are normally rubber mounted to the body, need their own separate earths so that their electrical components can function correctly.

Builders of custom or kit cars may have to modify this system slightly. GRP (fibreglass) body panels will not conduct electricity so they cannot be used as an earth connection. If the car has a steel chassis or subframes then these can be earthed to the battery (Fig 17).

Nearby components mounted on the GRP bodywork can then be earthed to these structures using short connecting leads (Fig 18).

If the car is an all GRP structure (I have owned three of these in the past) then the most convenient method is to arrange earthing points (I used long stainless steel bolts) connected directly to the battery, at convenient points around the vehicle and to earth nearby components to these. Remember, if you choose to earth a number of components through a single common wire it must be capable of carrying the total current for all of the shared components.

Whichever method you choose for your earth returns, try to position them within the vehicle so that they are not exposed to the elements. Clean, corrosion free, metal to metal contact is vital for them to work efficiently.

The subframe can then be used as an earthing point for various sections of the wiring harness.

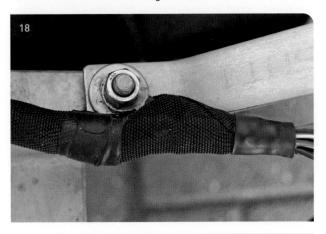

04 Components

All the individual items

The electrical system of a car is actually made up from a number of sub-systems each containing a number of components connected together. This chapter will look at the individual components which make up these sub-systems.

Ignition components

Two components essential to all spark ignition systems are the spark plug and the induction coil (ignition coil). The first commercially available spark plug was invented in 1902.

A modern spark plug with a fine wire Iridium electrode. The fine wire can produce a stronger spark from a lower voltage and the Iridium is resistant to erosion.

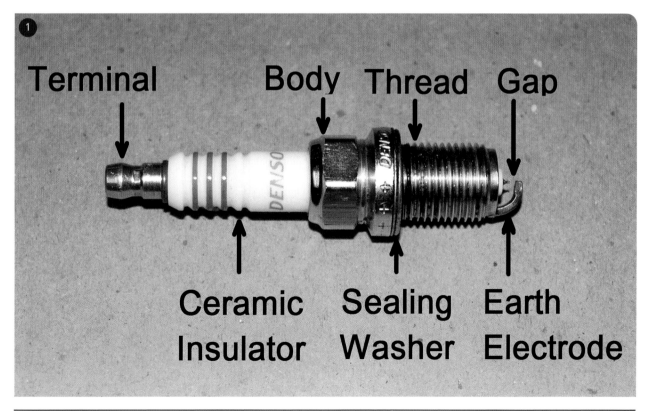

① Terminal   Body   Thread   Gap

Ceramic Insulator   Sealing Washer   Earth Electrode

Although spark plugs have changed a lot in detail since then, their basic construction has remained the same (Fig 1).

A high voltage spark jumps across the gap between the electrodes and the heat from this spark ignites the fuel mixture. In use, the electrodes gradually erode away but modern spark plugs are effectively maintenance free for 12,000 miles.

Typically around 20,000 volts is needed to produce a spark powerful enough to jump across the spark gap. An induction coil (or ignition coil) is used to convert the 12v supply from a car battery into the high voltage (HT) needed to ignite the fuel mixture at high pressure in the combustion chamber (Fig 2).

An induction coil works like a transformer. It has two coils of wire wound around a central soft iron core. One coil, called the primary, has a small number of turns of thick wire. The primary coil would have a resistance of around 3 ohms. The other coil, called the secondary, has thousands of turns of fine wire. The low voltage supply is passed through the primary coil, creating a magnetic field around both coils. The iron core concentrates the magnetic field. When the primary current is switched off, the magnetic field collapses. This causes a voltage pulse to be produced in the secondary coil which, because of the large number of turns in the secondary coil, is much higher, typically 20,000 volts.

A standard 12v ignition (induction) coil.

Contact breaker points. These are used to trigger the spark by switching off the current to the ignition coil at the correct moment.

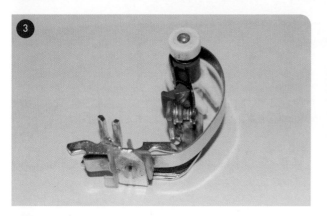

To produce a timed spark at exactly the right moment in a 4-stroke engine cycle, the switch controlling the ignition coil must be driven by, and timed to, the engine itself. This is achieved by the contact breakers or points which switch off the current in the primary coil winding and generate the spark at the exact moment required by the engine (Fig 3).

They were first used in magnetos.

Magnetos

A magneto is a complete ignition system in a single unit. It contains a generator, contact breaker, induction coil and condenser (Fig 4). It is driven from the engine by chain, gears or shaft, so the spark can be timed exactly.

Magnetos are simple, reliable and no external power source is needed. They are still used on mopeds, chainsaws and other engines where no battery is carried. Their main disadvantage is that the spark is weaker at low speed and when starting the engine, as the voltage produced depends on how fast the magento is turning.

The magneto is a self-contained ignition unit driven by the engine. No battery is required as it generates its own power.

Lucas distributor showing the contact breaker points, the cam which opens them and the condenser.

The condenser boosts the spark and also reduces arcing and erosion of the contact breaker surfaces.

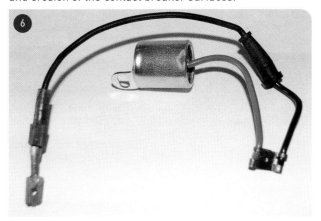

Battery powered ignition

As more cars began to use electric starting and lighting, a battery had to be carried to provide a constant source of electricity. Since the battery was there anyway, ignition systems were developed which used this battery voltage, switched on and off by engine driven contact breakers, to give exact spark timing. The constant battery voltage means the spark is strong at all engine speeds, overcoming the main disadvantage of the magneto. A later improvement was to use a ballast resistor and a 10v coil. For normal running, the resistor reduces the 12v battery voltage to suit the 10v coil. When starting the engine, the resistor is by-passed so the full 12v is fed to the coil producing a stronger spark still.

Mechanically timed ignition

Until recently most four-stroke engines have used a mechanically timed ignition system. The main component was the distributor which contained an engine driven rotating cam, a set of contact breaker points, a condenser, a rotor and a distributor cap (Fig 5).

As the engine turns, so does the cam inside the distributor. The points ride on the cam and, at the correct point in the engine cycle, the cam opens the breaker points to trigger the spark. The timing of the spark is adjusted by rotating the whole distributor body on its mountings.

The condenser or capacitor in the circuit (Fig 6) has two functions. It causes the magnetic field in the coil to collapse far quicker giving a much stronger spark, and it absorbs any reverse current generated in the coil which reduces sparking or arcing across the contact points.

An ignition schematic for a single cylinder engine is shown in figure 7.

Multi-cylinder engines need all of these components but also need a method of sending the high voltages produced by the coil to the individual spark plugs at the correct time. It is possible to produce a separate ignition system for each cylinder. My Suzuki 3-cylinder 2-stroke motorcycle had three sets of contact breakers and three separate ignition coils. The ignition timing was set individually for each cylinder. Although the Saab and Wartburg three-cylinder 2-stroke engines shared this system it is not really practical for automobile engines so a different system was developed. The high voltages generated by the coil are sent to the distributor

A single cylinder engine ignition schematic.

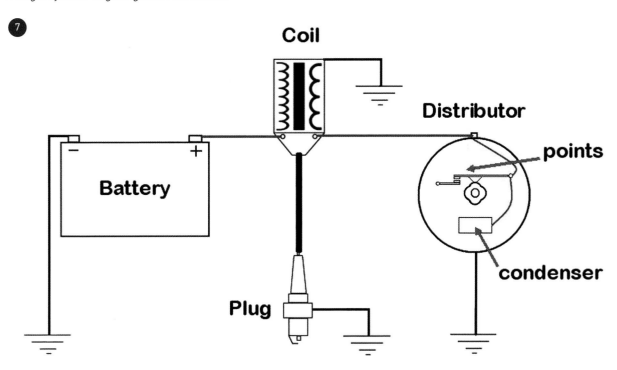

cap (Fig 8) mounted above the contact breakers and through to the rotor arm (Fig 9).

This is a rotating contact on the same shaft as the cam. As it rotates it connects the coil output to each spark plug lead in turn, in the correct sequence (Fig 10).

Ignition Timing

Ignition timing is normally measured as degrees of crankshaft rotation before the piston reaches the top of its stroke at Top Dead Centre. To extract the maximum power from the burning fuel it needs to be producing its maximum pressure just as the piston starts to move down the cylinder. The fuel/air mix takes a short but definite time to burn, so it needs to be ignited slightly earlier. Typically, at idle, the spark is fired 5 to10deg BTDC (before top dead centre).

Ignition advance

As engine speed increases, the fuel needs to be ignited earlier in order to have time to burn to reach maximum pressure. The ignition needs to be 'advanced', often by as much as 30deg measured at the crank. In a mechanical system this is done by bob weights, usually inside the distributor below the points, which move outwards under centrifugal force and rotate the operating cam on its shaft (Fig 11).

The weights and springs can be altered to tailor the advance curve, the way in which the ignition changes as the revs rise, to match the engine exactly.

The second method used to advance the ignition timing is called vacuum advance. It uses the vacuum present in the inlet manifold when cruising at part throttle to further advance the ignition timing, typically by up to 20deg. This generally increases fuel economy and driveability, particularly with weaker mixtures. A diaphragm connected to the inlet manifold moves the whole timing mechanism in the distributor (Fig 12).

A distributor cap for a 4-cylinder engine. The central carbon brush is connected to the coil and the four outer contacts connect to the spark plugs.

The rotor arm rotates inside the distributor cap and directs the high voltage to the correct spark plug.

A schematic showing how the high voltage (HT) is connected to each spark plug in turn in the correct firing sequence.

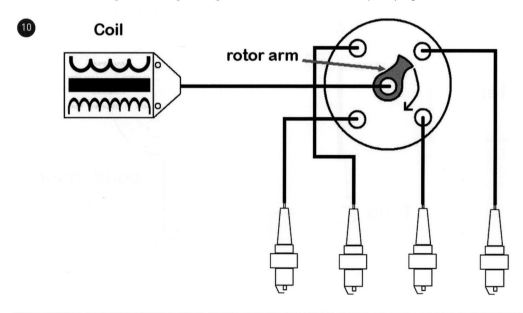

Limitations to mechanical ignition systems are...
- The contact breaker points need regular cleaning and the gap re-setting, or ignition timing varies and performance suffers.
- The useable current through the contact breakers is limited to around 5 amps. Higher currents cause arcing which destroys the contact surfaces. This limits the spark available at the plug.
- At higher revs the points can bounce on the cam when they close. This weakens the spark.
- At higher revs the points are closed for a very short time (dwell time) so the coil has very little time to build up its magnetic field and therefore produces a weaker spark. This problem is worse on 6 or 8-cylinder engines where more frequent sparks are required anyway. 8-cylinder engines often use twin contact breakers and coils.

In spite of these limitations, this system was used almost universally until the late 1970s, when electronic ignition systems started to appear.

Electronic ignition
Early transistor assisted systems still used points but they carried only a low trigger current which controlled the high primary current through a solid state transistor switching system. Very quickly, though, the points were replaced by an electronic switching system. Some used an optical trigger, where a rotor breaks a light beam, to trigger the spark (Fig 13).

Others used a Hall Effect sensor, which detects a rotating magnet or steel strip passing through a magnetic field (Fig 14).

A Lumenition switching system. A beam of light passing between the lenses is interrupted by the beam splitter to trigger the spark.

Lenses

Beam splitter

This Lucas system uses four metal pole pieces passing by a Hall sensor to trigger the spark.

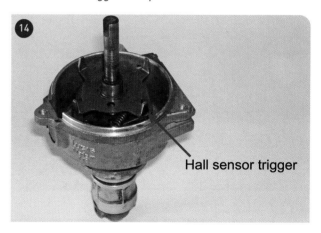

Hall sensor trigger

As the central shaft rotates faster the bob weights move outwards and move the cam on the shaft to advance the ignition.

A flexible diaphragm inside the capsule moves the back plate in the distributor to advance the ignition as the inlet manifold vacuum increases.

This Lucas ignition amplifier mounts to the outside of the distributor but they are now small enough to fit inside if required.

The sensor output triggers a solid state switching device such as a thyristor, which switches a large flow of current through the coil. The early ignition amplifiers were large units, often with cooling fins. Gradually they became smaller (Fig 15).

The latest aftermarket units actually fit inside the distributor itself. The coil, distributor and spark plugs are basically the same as the mechanical system, although coils designed for use with electronic ignition usually have a lower resistance (1.5) so that a higher current flows and a stronger spark is produced.

As well as removing all the servicing requirements and mechanical disadvantages of contact breakers, the higher current, rapid switching time and longer dwell period of a solid state switch produces a much more powerful and reliable spark.

Engine management

With the development of electronic fuel injection demanded by emission control legislation, it became logical to combine fuel control and ignition into one electronic system known as an Engine Management System (EMS) controlled by an Electronic Control Unit (ECU) (Fig 16).

An Engine Management System controls fuel delivery, ignition timing and firing order. Sensors on the engine measure engine speed, crankshaft position, airflow, throttle position, engine and air temperature, unused oxygen in the exhaust gases and other parameters (Fig 17/18/19).

The ECU compares these inputs with pre-loaded data or 'maps' in its memory then, along with many other functions, injects the correct amount of fuel and generates a spark at the ideal moment to burn it efficiently (Fig 20).

No distributor is used with these systems. The ECU triggers the coil pack or the spark plugs in the correct firing order (Fig 21). These systems can now produce upwards of 30,000 volts at the plugs.

Each coil in the pack normally fires two plugs simultaneously. In a 4-cylinder engine plugs one and three would share a coil and spark together. One spark would be wasted as one of the cylinders would be on its exhaust stroke when the plug fires but there are no disadvantages to this except slightly increased plug wear.

The latest systems use special spark plug caps which each contain their own individual ignition coil (Direct Ignition) (Fig 22).

This means high voltages are not carried around the

A Fiat ECU. Modern versions can be made much smaller than this.

The crank position sensor, as its name suggests, allows the ECU to determine the correct point to fire the ignition and inject the fuel for each cylinder.

The lambda sensor measures the amount of oxygen remaining in the exhaust gases and allows the ECU to adjust the amount of fuel injected.

This sensor measures engine coolant temperature and allows the ECU to adjust the ignition and fuelling accordingly.

This schematic shows the main sensors which provide data for the ECU and the main parameters which it controls as a result.

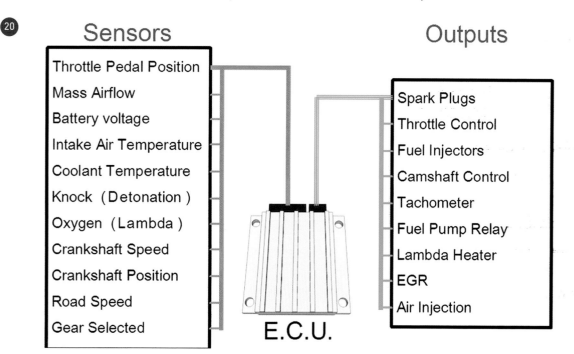

Sensors

- Throttle Pedal Position
- Mass Airflow
- Battery voltage
- Intake Air Temperature
- Coolant Temperature
- Knock (Detonation)
- Oxygen (Lambda)
- Crankshaft Speed
- Crankshaft Position
- Road Speed
- Gear Selected

E.C.U.

Outputs

- Spark Plugs
- Throttle Control
- Fuel Injectors
- Camshaft Control
- Tachometer
- Fuel Pump Relay
- Lambda Heater
- EGR
- Air Injection

engine. They are generated at the point where they are needed. Some cars mount all the direct ignition coils on a common bracket or 'rail' so they form a single unit over all the plugs.

Lights

Until very recently all vehicle electric lighting systems have used filament bulbs (incandescent light bulbs) (Fig 23). These consist of a coiled tungsten filament enclosed in a glass globe. The filament is connected to the external electrical contacts.

When electricity is passed through the filament it heats up to become white hot. At this point it emits visible light. Approximately 90% of the electricity consumed by a filament bulb is converted to heat and only 10% is available as useable

light. The tungsten filament reaches a temperature of around 3000degC (it melts at 3410degC). If there was any oxygen in the bulb the tungsten would burn away quickly, so the bulb is filled with an inert gas such as argon or krypton. This displaces the oxygen and will not react with the hot tungsten. In use, tungsten gradually evaporates from the filament and becomes deposited on the inside of the glass. The glass will slowly darken and the filament will eventually fail.

The power of a bulb is measured in watts. This is the electrical power it consumes and is not a direct measure of the light output, although it is a guide. A headlight bulb is typically 60w, indicators and brake lights are 21w and sidelight bulbs are around 5w. Bulbs also use a variety of mounting systems. The most common fittings are bayonet or screw in. Smaller bulbs can simply push into their fittings

A typical 4-cylinder coil pack. There are two separate coils each with twin outputs. Pairs of spark plugs are fired together.

A plug top coil. The actual ignition coil is contained within the plug cap. HT current is generated where it is needed not carried around the engine bay.

with no brass mounting collar. They are known as 'capless'.

Halogen bulbs contain a small amount of chlorine or iodine mixed with the inert gas. This produces a reversible chemical reaction which re-deposits any evaporated tungsten back onto the filament giving the bulb a longer service life and allowing the bulb to run at a higher temperature. To withstand this higher temperature the bulb is made from quartz or aluminosilicate glass, leading to

these bulbs commonly being called quartz-halogen.

In the 1990s High Intensity Discharge or HID lamps were developed. These have no filament. Instead an electric arc is passed through a mixture of the inert gas Xenon and vapourised metal halide salts (Fig 24).

They are much more efficient than filament bulbs and produce a much greater light output but have a much lower power consumption. They are not a straight swap for

A standard filament bulb. These are cheap and reliable but not very efficient.

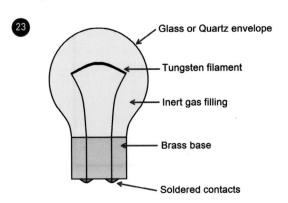

A simple inertia starter motor. A very high current is needed to turn over an engine fast enough for it to start.

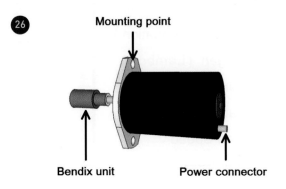

An HID capsule has no filament. The electric current passes through a mixture of Xenon and vapourised metal halides.

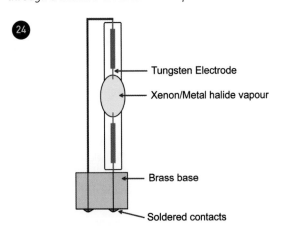

When the coil of the solenoid is energized the iron armature moves to close the contacts which carry the very high current for the starter motor.

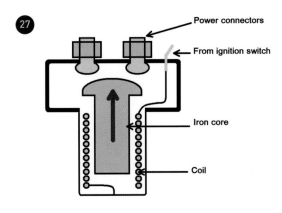

LEDs have a much longer life and a much lower current consumption than filament bulbs.

As the motor spins the Bendix unit is thrown into mesh with the flywheel ring gear. When the engine fires it is spun back again

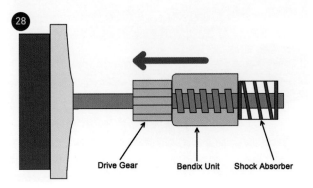

filament bulbs, although conversion kits are available. They need a higher voltage than the normal 12v car system and also need an ignitor rather like a fluorescent tube. Both these requirements are met by a ballast unit which controls the operation of the HID bulb. Replacing the very common H4 twin filament halogen headlamp bulb with an HID unit is a little trickier. The position of the two filaments within the bulb is critical to produce the correct main and dip beam patterns. Some H4 HID replacements only use an HID bulb for the main beam and use a conventional filament bulb for the dip beam. Others use a single HID bulb unit but use a solenoid to move the bulb within its housing to produce main and dip beams. These are known as Bi-xenon.

LED lights

Light Emitting Diodes became a practical proposition in the '60s. Red was the first commercially available colour followed by greens, blues and yellows in the '70s. The white light LED is a very recent development, becoming commercially available in the late '90s. Over this period the light output has increased dramatically too. The latest LEDs produce 10 times more light output per watt than a filament bulb and have even surpassed fluorescent tubes too (Fig 25).

LEDs have many advantages over filament bulbs. They are more robust, they have much lower energy consumption. They have a longer working life and are far more compact. These properties make them ideal for vehicle lighting and they are quickly replacing filament bulbs in all lighting and warning lamp applications. At the time of writing Audi has just produced a light unit using LEDs for main and dip headlight beams too.

If you choose to use LED indicators, their low current consumption means that a normal bi-metal strip flasher unit will not work. An electronic flasher unit will be required to operate them correctly.

Starter motor

An electric motor is constructed in basically the same way as a generator but works in reverse. Instead of using movement to produce electricity it uses electricity to produce movement (Fig 26).

A current is passed through coils suspended in a magnetic field and the coils move to turn the motor shaft. A

The pre-engaged starter unit has the solenoid mounted on top of the motor. The drive gear is engaged with the flywheel before it begins to turn.

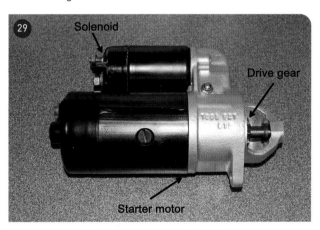

This rack and pinion system was used on British cars for many years. The rack and the pinion gears can be rotated to even out wear..

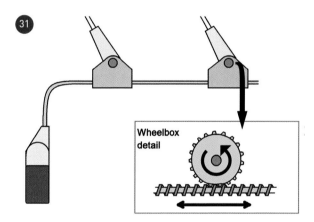

As the solenoid is energized it pulls the pivoted operating lever. This pushes the drive gear into mesh with the flywheel before the motor begins to spin.

The lever and crank system is easier and cheaper to manufacture but takes up more space in operation.

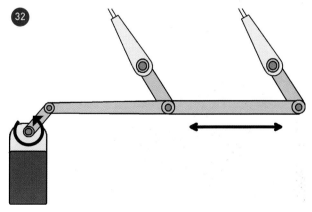

lot of power is needed to turn a car engine, especially on a cold day when the oil is viscous. To generate this power a high current is required, which is why starter motor cables are so thick. The current is also too big to be carried by a normal switch. Instead, the current is switched by a solenoid which closes heavy duty contacts (Fig 27). It is basically a high current relay.

The drive gear on the starter motor engages with the teeth of the ring gear on the outer rim of the flywheel. Once the engine starts the gear has to disengage to avoid damage to the motor and the ring gear. Early starters used an inertia gear which moved into mesh as the starter motor first spun and moved out when the engine fired (Fig 28).

The Bendix gear is noisy and eventually causes damage to

A car heater is basically a small radiator with a fan to provide the airflow if required.

A Revotec radiator cooling fan and thermostatic switch. The fan will only switch on when the coolant temperature rises above a pre-set level.

the ring gear teeth, so most modern starter motors are of the pre-engaged type where the solenoid is mounted on the motor (Fig 29) and moves the drive gear into mesh with the ring gear before it connects the electrical contacts (Fig 30).

Windscreen wipers
Although some pre-1950 systems used windscreen wipers which were operated by the engine's inlet manifold vacuum, all modern systems are powered by electric motors. Most are now multi-speed too.

There are two basic drive systems. The early Lucas system uses a flexible toothed rack moving backwards and forwards in a tube to drive the wiper arms through pinions mounted in wheel boxes on the bodywork (Fig 31).

The alternative system uses a crank on the motor to operate a pantograph system of pivoted rods which move the wiper arms (Fig 32).

Heater motor
A car heater uses hot water from the engine cooling system passing through a small radiator or heat exchanger to heat the air entering the car. When the car is moving the air flows naturally through the unit and is warmed as it enters the car. When the car is stationary or if a boost is required, a fan, driven by a small electric motor, is used to draw air through the heat exchanger (Fig 33). Modern cars use multi-speed heater fans. This is normally achieved by using various resistors to reduce the current flowing through the fan to produce the slower speeds.

Radiator fan
Engine driven cooling fans are noisy, they sap engine power and they produce their lowest air flow when they are actually needed most, when the car is idling in traffic. Electric cooling fans are a far better proposition (Fig 34).

They are normally controlled by a thermostatic switch, so they are only switched on when they are needed, making them far more efficient. They draw a high current so they should be wired using a relay.

The coil and contacts cause the iron core and diaphragm to vibrate making the required sound.

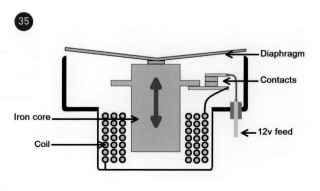

The heating and cooling of the bi-metal strip causes the contacts to open and close. This switches the current off and on causing the indicators to flash.

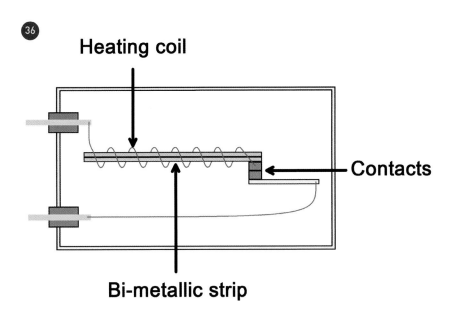

36

Heating coil

Contacts

Bi-metallic strip

Horn

IVA regulations apply to this component so check carefully. Air horns, as the name suggests, have an electrically driven compressor to blow air through the horn unit. The normal electric horn units (Fig 35) have a 'make and break' contact breaker unit similar to the one in a domestic electric doorbell. An electromagnet attracts an iron armature which is connected to a diaphragm. As the armature moves it opens the contacts, switches off the current and returns to its original position. This cycle is repeated many times a second causing the diaphragm to vibrate and generate the horn sound.

In addition to these basic components modern cars may have luxuries such as central locking, electric windows, electric mirrors and so on but they are all operated by variations of the systems described here.

Flasher Units

The indicators on a motor vehicle are supposed to flash 1-2 times per second. For many years this was achieved using a very simple unit incorporating a bi-metallic strip and a heating coil (Fig 36). A bi-metallic strip is made from two thin strips of different metals bonded together. If the strip is heated the two metals expand at different rates causing the strip to bend. In a flasher unit the current flowing to the indicators passes through a small heating coil wrapped around the bi-metallic strip. When the strip gets hot it bends and opens the circuit. This switches off the current to the indicators and the heating coil. The strip cools down, straightens out and re-connects the circuit again. This cycle is repeated as long as the indicators are switched on.

If one of the indicator bulbs fails a much lower current flows round the circuit, so the heating coil takes much longer to warm up. The remaining indicator bulb flashes much more slowly or stays on constantly. This is a design feature of the flasher unit to warn the driver of the bulb failure.

A hazard warning flasher unit is constructed slightly differently. All four indicator bulbs flash together, so the flasher unit needs to carry a higher current. In addition, since this is a warning signal, the flash rate must stay constant even if one or more bulbs fail. To achieve this the heating coil is powered independently of the current flowing to the bulbs (Fig 37).

The latest flasher units are electronic and use solid state timers to produce a constant flash rate regardless of the type of bulbs fitted and their current draw.

To ensure a constant flash rate the heating coil is wired independently from the lighting circuit producing a constant current flow through the coil.

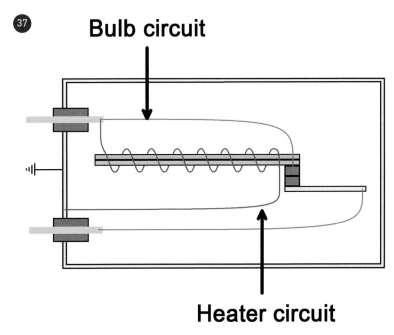

37

Bulb circuit

Heater circuit

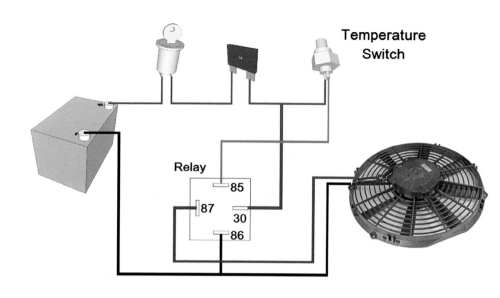

Temperature Switch

Relay
85
87
30
86

05 Controls

Switches, rheostats and relays

A switch is basically a component which can conveniently open or close an electric circuit to prevent or allow the current to flow. Inside the switch are contacts which are bridged by a conductor to complete the circuit as the switch is operated. The contact material is chosen for its conductivity, its wear resistance and its resistance to corrosion. Contacts are often coated with a thin layer of gold to prevent corrosion and switches normally incorporate a wiping action as they open and close to keep the contacts clean.

Switches are described by their actuator and by their function. The actuator is the moving part of the switch which is operated by the user. It can be a toggle, a rocker, a push button or a rotating knob (Fig 1-4).

Toggle switches are less popular for automotive use now as the IVA regulations do not allow their unguarded use in areas where they could be impacted by the driver in an accident. Rocker switches are preferred.

Rocker switches. These have built-in warning lights.

A typical toggle switch. IVA regulations restrict the use of this type of switch.

A high quality aluminium billet push switch. This one has screw in connectors.

Rotary switches styled to suit vintage or classic cars.

The function of a switch depends on the number of poles (moveable contacts) and throws (movements) in its operation. A simple on/off switch would have one set of contacts and two positions for the actuator, off and on. This would be a Single Pole Single Throw switch (SPST) (Fig 5).

By adding a second set of contacts a changeover switch can be produced. This would be a Single Pole Double Throw switch (SPDT) (Fig 6). It still has two positions, but they are both 'on'. The power is switched between Circuit 1 and Circuit 2. A headlamp dip switch is an example of this type.

A variation of this switch has an off position in the centre. This is called a Single Pole Triple Throw or a Single Pole Centre Off switch.

For more complex functions multiple switches can be built into the same casing.

A schematic for a Single Pole Single Throw (SPST) switch.

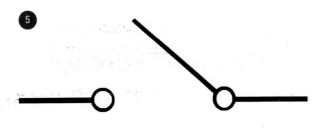

A schematic for a Single Pole Double Throw (SPDT) switch.

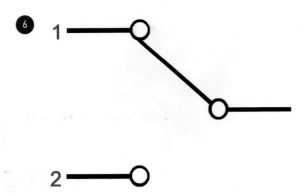

A Double Pole Single Throw (DPST) switch is effectively two separate switches operated by the same actuator (Fig 7).

A Double Pole Double Throw (DPDT) switch is two separate changeover switches operated by a common actuator (Fig 8).

Most switches are of the 'latching' type. They lock into position when the actuator is operated and remain there until switched off again. Less common are the switches known as 'momentary'. Their contacts are connected as long as the actuator is held in position but they spring open as soon as it is released. These switches are used for windscreen washers, electric windows and motorised mirrors. Momentary switches can also be used in conjunction with a latching relay. This allows them to

A schematic for a Double Pole Single Throw (DPST) switch. Basically two SPST switches coupled together.

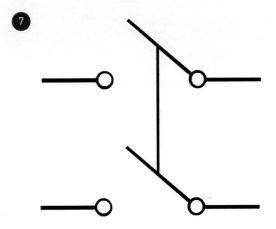

A schematic for a Double Pole Double Throw (DPDT) switch. Basically two SPDT switches on a common actuator

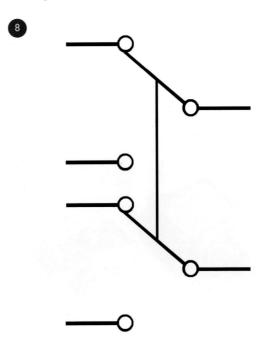

The internals of a rheostat. As the wiper moves around the carbon track the resistance between the centre and outer connectors varies.

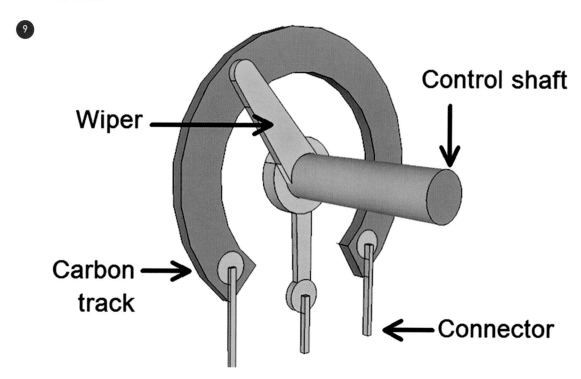

9

Wiper

Control shaft

Carbon track

Connector

replace a latching switch. When the switch is pressed for the first time the relay is energised and latches on. When the switch is pressed again the relay unlatches and switches off.

Not all switches in a car are driver operated. Interior light switches are operated automatically when the doors open, and temperature controlled thermostatic switches turn on electric radiator fans when required. There are various warning lights in modern cars which are switched on by sensors around the vehicle and some prestige cars have wipers and lights which switch on in response to rain or light levels.

The internal construction of an automotive relay. The terminals are numbered on a standard system.

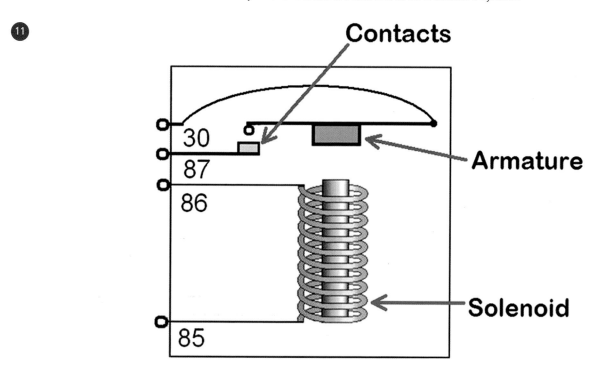

11

Contacts

Armature

Solenoid

30

87

86

85

The standard pin layout of a relay as viewed from the base.

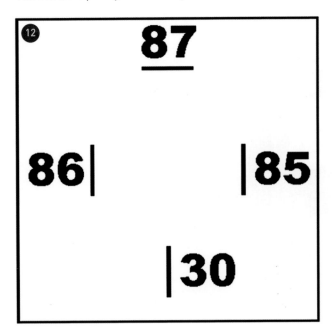

Rheostats

A rheostat is a variable resistor. Its resistance can be increased or decreased usually be either rotating or sliding a control knob. They are used in volume controls on audio equipment and in dimmer switches for lights. The resistance material is either a carbon track or a long coil of nichrome wire. The resistance is varied by moving a contact or 'wiper' along the material so that more or less of it is included in the circuit (Fig 9).

Rheostats have limited use in vehicles as they do not have the capacity to carry much current. They are used in dimmers for instrument lighting and in the sender unit for fuel gauges. In high current applications, such as multi-speed heater fans, fixed high current resistors are switched in and out of the circuit to vary the current.

Relays

Whenever switch contacts open or close a small electric spark is produced. This is known as 'arcing'. This process will slowly erode away the contact surfaces and eventually cause the switch to fail. The higher the current flowing through the switch the more destructive the arcing will be. Switches designed to carry higher currents will have bigger more robust contact surfaces but will still eventually fail due to arcing. For this reason all switches have a specified maximum current rating and a minimum operating life. For instance...

Rating - 2A 250Vac, 6A 125Vac
Life – 20,000 on/off cycles at full load

The modern trend is to use smaller lighter switches in the car and to protect them by using relays to carry the heavy currents. A relay is an electrically operated switch. The actuator is an electromagnet or solenoid which only needs a small current to operate. The electromagnet attracts an iron

This is a typical circuit operating an electric radiator fan. These fans draw a high current through the thermostatic switch leading to arcing and damage to the contacts.

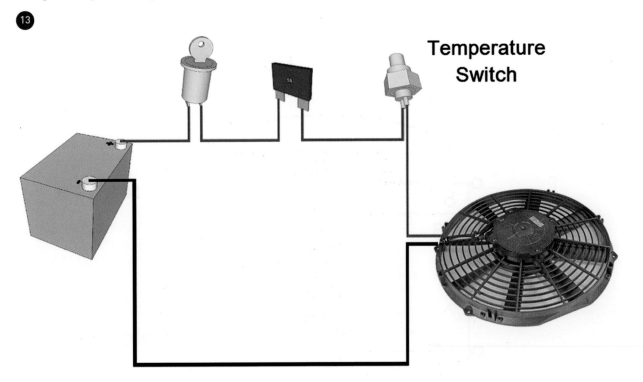

Temperature
Switch

In this modified circuit the relay carries the high current drawn by the fan and the thermostatic switch only carries the small current needed to energise the relay solenoid.

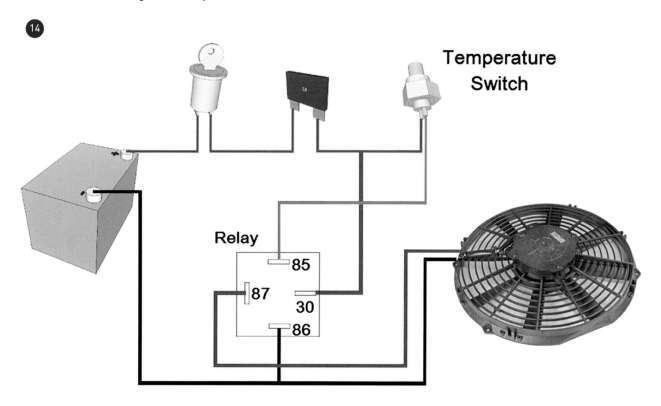

14

armature which closes the main switch contacts to carry the heavy current (Fig 11).

The pins on a relay are numbered using a standard system and are arranged on the actual relay in a standard format (Fig 12).

In use, the main switch carries only the small current required to energise the solenoid, so arcing is greatly reduced and the service life of the switch is greatly extended.

Wiring a relay is quite straightforward but it does need an extra power supply. The normal live output from the car switch is connected to pin 85 to energise the solenoid. The additional power supply is connected to pin 30 and the live output from the relay to the component is taken from pin 87.

Using a relay in a circuit does make the wiring a little more complex but if they are designed in from the start it is no real problem. An electric radiator fan is a high current item often drawing upwards of 15A, so the thermostatic switch in the cooling system can be damaged by the arcing resulting from switching this high current. A relay added to the circuit will prevent this, giving the switch a much longer service life (Fig 13/14).

A useful variation to the standard relay is the changeover version which is the equivalent of a SPDT switch. It is ideal for switching between main and dip beams on high powered headlamps (Fig 15/16).

Automotive relays have standard 6mm male blade

connectors so the wires can be connected directly to the terminals but it is sometimes easier to use a relay socket or relay box (Fig 17). The sockets usually have some provision

The power feed on terminal 30 is switched between the two output terminals 87 and 87a as the solenoid is switched on and off.

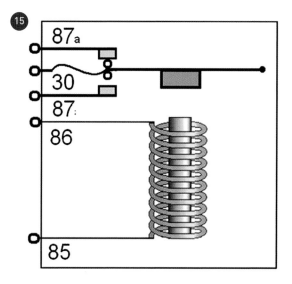

15

for panel mounting and the relays simply plug into the sockets allowing quick and easy replacement.

Switches are an essential component in a motor vehicle and are available in a wide variety of styles and configurations, from vintage replicas to ultra-modern aluminium billet push-button units with built in illumination and warning lights. They are also subject to the IVA regulations in newly built cars, so check these before you make your final selection. Always use good quality switches. They will have a longer service life and a smoother operation in use. I would also suggest that any switch which will carry more than 2 or 3 amps (25-35 watts power) should be protected by a relay. In the next chapter I will continue with the dashboard theme and look in more detail at instrumentation and displays.

The standard pin layout of a changeover relay as viewed from the base.

Relay sockets showing the mounting holes. These sockets clip together to form a convenient relay box.

06 Cockpit Displays

Warning lights and instruments

It is interesting that as the reliability of vehicle components, and engines in particular, has increased massively, so has the number of warning lights and status indicators telling us when something has failed. If you are restoring an older vehicle it is possible that the cockpit display will consist of just a speedometer and a few warning lights for ignition, oil pressure and indicators. Upmarket cars may have an ammeter and an oil pressure gauge to supplement the warning lights, but are still not lavishly equipped by today's standards.

If you are designing your own dashboard then there is now a huge range of gauges, warning lights and electronic displays to suit any style of car. You can choose to fit separate gauges with either analogue or digital displays. If you are short of space there are gauges which combine two or more functions in the same casing or, ultimately, there are digital dashboards which combine the functions of a full set of

gauges along with data logging facilities should you wish to use them. Once again, the IVA regulations apply to certain instruments and warning lights, so if you are building a kit or custom car which will need to be registered on completion, make sure you check the relevant sections of the manual.

Types of display
The three most commonly used types of displays in a vehicle are buzzers, lights and gauges.

Audible warnings
Buzzers and beepers are used sparingly in motor vehicles. To avoid distracting the driver they are really only employed when the vehicle is stationary or moving slowly. They are used in reversing alarms to warn both the driver and, in the case of HGVs, pedestrians in the area. They are also used in

These small bulbs are very fragile and can be difficult to replace when they burn out.

A rocker switch with a built in warning light and legend.

①

②

seatbelt warning systems and finally you may also find an option for an audible warning when using your indicators (generally used when the indicator has no self cancelling mechanism).

Lights

Lights only have two possible states. They can be on or off. This makes them ideal to quickly and clearly indicate the status of a system or to provide a warning. Status indicator lights inform or remind the driver whether a system is switched on or off. Examples include heated rear windows, main beam, fog lights etc. It is possible to buy switches with interchangeable legends and integral status lights built into them (Fig 1).

These can be very useful as they can save space in the dash area, simplify the wiring (as no separate light is needed) and, if selected carefully, can also comply with whatever regulations are applicable.

Warning lights alert the driver to a fault or a dangerous condition. Ignition warning, brake fluid level or seatbelt lights are examples of this type of indicator. At the time of writing, warning lights for main beam, indicators, brake fluid level and reversing lights (if not on an automatic switch) are compulsory, but check current regulations to be sure. In the

past, warning lights have used small filament bulbs of around 2w output to provide the illumination (Fig 2), along with coloured lenses to give the traditional red, blue, green and amber lights (Fig 3).

When these bulbs blow they can be difficult to replace due to poor access behind the dashboard area. You may prefer to use LEDs instead when you wire your car. They have a longer service life, use less current and need no lens to produce their colour (Fig 4).

A normal LED only needs a supply voltage of 2v-3v but for automotive use they are supplied with a built in resistor to enable them to be connected directly to a 12v supply. They can also be obtained with a built-in flasher circuit should you need it.

If you decide to use an LED for the ignition warning light and your car is equipped with an alternator, you will need to make a slight modification to the wiring. To understand this you need to know a little about how the alternator works.

Car alternators do not use a permanent magnet. Instead the rotor is a spinning electromagnet which can be varied in strength to control the output of the alternator. When the ignition is switched on a small current (around 0.2 A) flows from the battery and ignition switch through the ignition

The colours and legends are formed by the lenses on the warning lights.

LED lights are more robust and use less current. These are suitable for a 12v supply.

The ignition light is an essential part of the circuit. Current flows through it to power the alternator field coils on start up.

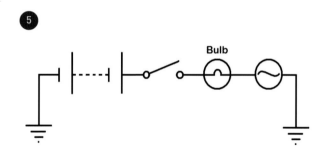

An LED does not flow enough current to excite the alternator field coils so a resistor is wired in parallel to perform this function.

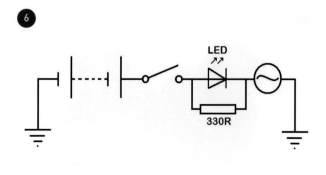

warning light to the alternator field coils to energise them (Fig 5). The ignition warning light illuminates whilst this current is flowing.

Once the alternator is spinning its output is directed to the battery to charge it and to the field coils to keep them energised (Self Excitation). The warning light goes out at this point since the full alternator output is connected to both sides of the bulb at the same time so no current flows. The ignition warning lamp is therefore an essential part of the charging circuit and should it ever blow it is very unlikely that the alternator will charge unless there is a small amount of residual magnetism left in the rotor.

An LED uses a much smaller current (0.02A) than a filament bulb and this is not enough to energise the alternator field coils, so if you choose to use an LED for your ignition light you need to provide an alternative current supply for the rotor windings. This is easily done by wiring a 330Ω – 470Ω resistor in parallel with the LED light (Fig 6).

The current flowing through both components together will allow the alternator to function correctly. The resistor needs to have a power rating of around 1w to safely carry the current without overheating.

This aftermarket warning light cluster is available in a number of formats for kit and custom car builders. It is mounted and wired as a single unit.

Using the engine to earth the circuit through the switch means that only a single wire is needed for this oil pressure light to operate.

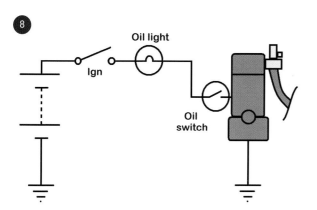

Modern cars tend to mount their warning lights as a cluster rather than individual units. If this is the way you want to go, there are options available to you. If you are looking for something with more contemporary styling that is also compliant with current regulations there is a warning light set which is available as a straight bar or as a T-shaped unit (Fig 7).

Any of these pre-assembled units are simple to mount and will simplify the wiring by having a common earth wire for the whole unit.

This brake wear indicator circuit needs no switch. The circuit is completed by a conductor moulded into the brake friction material.

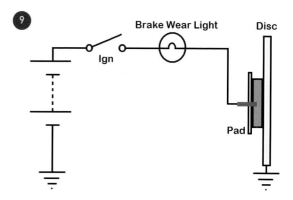

There is a wide range of available instruments. Not all of them will be applicable or desirable in your vehicle..

Warning light switches

To switch on a warning light all that is needed is a simple SPST switch which can be operated by whichever parameter is being monitored.

An oil pressure warning light switch, for example, is screwed into the main oil gallery of the engine. The engine oil pressure acts on a spring-loaded diaphragm, keeping the switch contacts open. If the oil pressure falls below a preset level the spring pushes on the diaphragm and closes the contacts to switch on the warning light. Some of these switches have a setting which allows the oil pressure to drop to a dangerously low level (5 psi) before warning the driver. If available, it is worth fitting a 'competition' oil switch which will operate at a much higher pressure (20-25 psi) instead. Engine-mounted switches tend to have only one connecting wire. The live feed goes through the warning light to the switch and the earth return is made through the engine block and the engine earthing strap (Fig 8).

A low fluid warning light will normally use a switch which is operated by a float mechanism. When the fluid level is high, the switch contacts are kept open by the float mechanism but if the fluid level falls and the float drops, the switch contacts close to switch on the light.

Brake wear warning lights do not use a separate switch.

Instead a wire or conductor is moulded into the pad material a set distance below the surface. The warning light circuit is connected to this wire. When the pad material wears to the specified depth, the conductor rubs against the disc and completes the circuit to earth, causing the light to switch on (Fig 9).

In general, warning light switches are simple and reliable. Sender units for gauges, however, tend to be more complex

Digital dash units are becoming increasingly popular.

A combination of digital and analogue can be combined to good effect, as per these top specification Stack units.

Here's an interesting mix, with white faced dials with modern pointers and bezels mounted to good effect on a carbon dashboard.

Black faces with white lettering looks good in vintage or classic cars.

More lurid colours are also available, and note that these units are also personalised for the make of car.

as they are required to send a constantly varying signal to a gauge in response to a variable condition within the vehicle.

Gauges

There are some parameters in a motor vehicle which operate over a whole range of values or conditions and the driver needs to know a numerical or at least a comparative value for these. A simple on-off indicator is no use here. We need an instrument capable of displaying constantly varying values. The most obvious example of the requirement for an accurate numerical reading is the speedometer. In the UK a speedometer is compulsory. It should not read less than the true speed and has to be accurate to within 10 per cent. It must also be driven from the vehicle. It cannot be GPS based.

A fuel gauge is a good example of a parameter which really only needs a comparative value. We do not necessarily need to know the exact number of gallons or litres of fuel in the tank but it is useful to know if the tank is full, half full or almost empty.

Some gauges or readouts complement or improve on existing warning lights. An oil pressure gauge enables the driver to constantly monitor the engine oil pressure rather than relying on a light to inform them of a fault. Similarly an ammeter will indicate not just whether the battery is being

Something more traditional here. Note the array of different switches and buttons, too.

This instrument combines a speedometer, rev counter and clock into one small unit.

charged, but by how much. This will highlight any problems with over charging as well as under charging.

There is a huge range of gauges available (Fig 10). Not all of them will be relevant or applicable to your car. Unless you have a turbocharger on your vehicle, for example, a boost pressure gauge will be a complete waste of money. A gauge which logs engine running time is very useful on a race car but much less so on a normal road car. Think carefully about the gauges you need to fit in your car.

The gauges vary in style too. Black faces with white

A complete digital dash unit is augmented with yet further analogue and digital gauges to good effect.

All the current flowing to and from the battery must go through the ammeter for it to read correctly. Heavy duty wiring is needed.

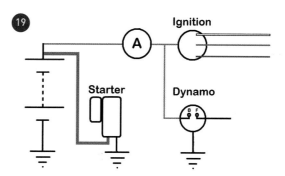

The voltmeter is simply connected in parallel with the ignition circuit and carries only a very small current.

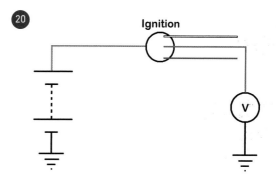

lettering are traditional (Fig 11) but this combination is often reversed for competition gauges. Magnolia faced dials suit the look of a classic car very well.

The sizes for dials and gauges have been reasonably well standardised but there is still some variation. Minor instruments tend to be 52mm in diameter but the major instruments such as the speedometer and tachometer can be 100mm or 80mm overall.

40 years ago the words digital and analogue meant very little to most people. Today they are in common use to describe almost any sort of display. The traditional automotive instruments were obviously analogue but nowadays, not surprisingly, are also available with digital readouts or displays (Fig 13).

If space is at a premium on your dash it is possible to buy gauges with two instruments built into a single casing. The increasing miniaturisation of electronic components has made it possible to combine a number of functions into a single instrument (Fig 17).

The modern trend for production cars is to produce an entire dashboard as a single unit with gauges, indicators and warning lights integrated into the one component (Fig 18). In the last few years this has also become an option for custom and kit car builders too.

As you can see there is a tremendous choice of instrumentation available to you and obviously the choice is entirely up to you. It will depend on the style of car you are building, its intended use, your personal taste and, of course, your budget. I can offer you some advice based on my own experience though. My tastes tend to be towards the traditional. I prefer analogue instruments for their looks and their practicality. They can be read at a glance. All you really need to see is whether the needle is roughly in the correct place on the dial. How often do you actually need to know whether your engine oil pressure is exactly 63 or 64 psi? A digital instrument, on the other hand, has to actually be read carefully to see whether the indicated value is in the acceptable range. Racers tend to use analogue gauges for this reason and they also rotate them in the dashboard so that when all the parameters are correct all the needles are pointing vertically upwards. This enables them to read the whole dash at a glance and to easily spot any reading which is not correct.

I tend not to go for overkill with my instrumentation. A

A mechanical oil pressure gauge. As the pressure increases it expands along the tube and operates the gauge.

A Smiths voltage stabiliser designed to supply some of their gauges. The unit must be mounted and earthed correctly. Terminal 'B' is the 12v input (Battery), Terminal 'I' feeds the instruments with a stabilised 10v.

The electric oil pressure sender is quite bulky as it uses a variable resistor operated by a spring loaded diaphragm to measure the oil pressure.

If you wish to fit an oil pressure gauge and retain the oil light switch a 'T' piece is needed. The threads must match the engine and sender units.

This is my GTM dash panel with the cardboard discs which I used to position the instruments correctly. A sheet of melamine faced board ready for use.

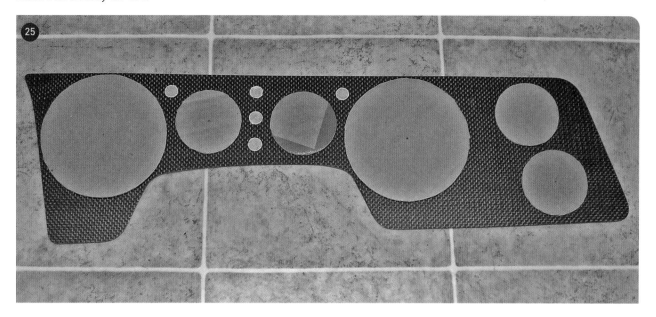

speedometer is compulsory by law. I also regard a tachometer as essential in anything which might be considered a sporting car. The minor instruments I always fit are a fuel gauge, a water temperature gauge, an oil pressure gauge and a voltmeter (battery condition meter). The latter two instruments are used alongside the existing warning lights not instead of them. If you have a dynamo charging system, an ammeter is a better choice than a voltmeter. It gives you more information about the operation of the system. If you have an alternator, as most modern cars do, they normally charge even when the engine is idling and the solid state control system reacts so quickly and so efficiently that an ammeter becomes less useful and a voltmeter is a better choice. Voltmeters are also easier to wire in.

An ammeter must be wired in series into the main power line so that all the power except the starter motor current passes through it. It carries currents of 30A or more so the wiring needs to be substantial.

A voltmeter on the other hand is wired to the output of the ignition switch and carries only a very small current to give a voltage reading.

By now you may be thinking that you are close to making your final choice of the instruments you wish to fit to your car, but there is still a further decision to be made. Some types of instruments can be driven either electronically or mechanically. A mechanically driven instrument will have a cable, a pressure tube or a thin capillary tube connecting it to its drive gears or sender unit (Fig 21).

An electrically driven instrument is simply connected by wires to its sender unit but the sender unit itself is more complicated as it must convert changes in temperature, pressure or movement to electrical signals which the gauge can display (Fig 22).

A speedometer is a good example of a gauge available in both mechanical and electrical forms. Until recently they were normally driven by a flexible cable connected to the car wheel or to the gearbox. Electronically driven speedometers are now readily available and they use sensors connected to a driveshaft or a disc brake to generate a signal which can be used to measure speed. In the case of cars equipped with ABS it is possible to use the ABS wheel speed sensor to drive the speedometer too.

Some electronic gauges operate by measuring the current flowing through a sender unit using a bi-metal strip and heating coil. This gives a very stable reading but also makes them sensitive to the overall voltage of the system. On older systems the overall voltage would drop if the headlights and window heaters were in use causing these gauges to read low. To overcome this the gauges were designed to operate on a lower voltage, often around 10v and were powered through a crude voltage stabiliser which could provide a constant supply voltage to the gauges even when the main supply was under high demand (Fig 23). Smith's fuel and temperature gauges used this system.

Whichever type of gauge you decide to use you must also use the matching sender unit supplied by the gauge manufacturer. Not only do different manufacturers use different physical fittings on their units but the electronics will match too. Oil pressure and water temperature senders may need adaptors to enable them to be screwed into the fittings in your particular cylinder or head (Fig 24).

Many different thread types and sizes are used. In the UK we tend to use BSP threads and fittings, the USA use NPT and of course European and Japanese manufacturers use Metric sizes. You will also find that some threads are parallel and others have a taper to ensure a fluid tight seal. You may also need a 'T' piece if you wish to retain the warning light

This is the dash panel with the instruments and warning lights fitted in the positions determined using the cardboard discs.

switch when you fit an oil pressure gauge.

Whatever your final selection, make sure that you get the correct combination of senders, fittings and adaptors for your specific application.

Finally you need to think about the positioning of your instruments, lights and controls. In small cars there is a restricted amount of space to mount gauges in your direct eye line and small steering wheels can make the problem even worse. If this is the case you need to prioritise your instruments so that the most important ones, the speedo and rev counter are in clear view with the rest positioned so that they can be checked regularly. The same applies to important

warning lights such as the ignition, oil, main beam or indicator lights. These should be positioned so that they will be instantly noticed when they illuminate. The best way to achieve this is to temporarily fit the dashboard, seats and steering wheel into the car then to cut out some paper or cardboard discs of the correct size to represent the instruments and lights. Blu-Tak can be used to re-position these discs on the dashboard until the best positions are found then the instruments can be permanently mounted (Fig 25/26).

Make a good job of your dashboard. It is the part of the car you will spend the most time looking at and needs to be designed to work well and to be aesthetically pleasing too.

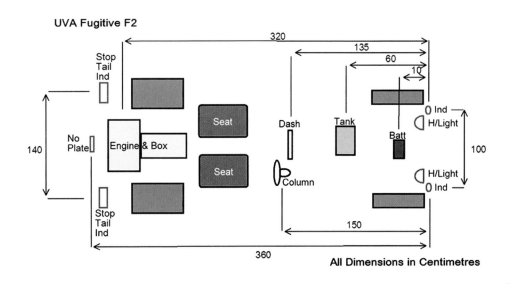

UVA Fugitive F2

All Dimensions in Centimetres

07 Planning The Wiring

Positioning and routing

Before you can even begin to think about cutting wires and attaching connectors you have a number of decisions to make. You need to decide what systems you will fit into your car, which components you will use and where every component will be positioned in the vehicle. You can add additional components or accessories at a later date, even after the car is complete and running, but it will be much easier and the finished result will be much neater if you wire in everything you need from the start.

Initial decisions

If you are rewiring a classic or standard vehicle then most of these initial decisions will have been made for you, but if you are wiring a kit or custom car from scratch you will have to think them through carefully. There are certain areas where you have no choice. Some systems are mandated by the IVA regulations. You must have a brake fluid warning light with a testing circuit, for example. Lighting requirements are very specific and even the types of switches you can use are limited by the regulations. Read them carefully before you begin so that you don't find yourself making last minute modifications at the IVA testing station (see Appendix 1 for more information).

For all the other areas, though, you have a fairly free choice and the systems you choose to fit will obviously depend on the type of vehicle you have and its intended use. If you have a sports car or vintage car with no screen you will obviously not need a wiper system or a demister and will probably choose not to fit a heater either. You can choose whether or not you want an audio system, electric windows, interior light, electric cooling fan and so on.

Once you have decided which systems you intend to fit, the next step is to select the actual components you will be using in the vehicle. Some of these may be taken from the donor car or the car you are modifying; others will need to be obtained from other sources. There are a number of companies specialising in auto electrical supplies now. You will find their contact details in the appendices. You need to select the actual components because you need to know details about how they will be mounted, what type of connectors they require and where the connectors are positioned on the units.

Ideally you should then obtain the actual components you intend to use and mount or temporarily locate them in the car in their final positions and alignments. It is so frustrating to trim wires to length and attach the connectors only to find out at a later date that you need to move or rotate a

I designed the fusebox of my GTM Coupe to flip down below the dashboard for easy access. It was secured by quick release Dzus fasteners.

component and the wires are no longer long enough to reach. If you are unable to use the actual components for any reason then you can attach labels or masking tape to the body or chassis of the car showing the intended position and alignment of the missing items.

Component selection

If you are rewiring a car as part of a strict restoration project, then the components you will be using will be serviceable original parts, reconditioned components, new old stock, direct replacements, or modern replicas of the original parts. They should fit and function as well or better than the originals and a standard wiring loom should connect them all up nicely according to the factory wiring diagram. If you are uprating, customising or building a new car you may be using some of the original components, such as the generator, ignition system or engine management, but you will also be selecting a large number of new parts according to your own personal preferences. If your car will be subject to an IVA test before you can use it, then you need to carefully read the relevant sections of the IVA manual to establish which components are acceptable before you spend any money.

I would not presume to tell you which specific lights, switches or gauges to buy for your car. That is entirely up to you and, judging by some of the cars I am now seeing at shows and meetings, my taste in styling certainly leans towards the 'traditional' (some would say old fashioned) rather than the modern LED based digital styling which is becoming much more commonplace nowadays.

My advice on component selection is to buy high quality components wherever possible. As mentioned previously, the majority of vehicle breakdowns are caused by electrical rather than mechanical failure and the increasing complexity of electrical systems is hardly likely to improve this situation. Dirty or corroded connections are a common cause of failure so it is worth paying a slight premium for waterproof plugs and sockets in areas where water ingress is a possibility. High quality switches will operate with a smoother more positive action and will have a longer service life. Proper automotive light clusters should be waterproof and should have good quality bulb holders and connectors whereas the cheaper units, often designed primarily for use on trailers, may allow water to leak inside and will have poorer quality internals.

LEDs may be a good choice for warning lights and minor illumination. They are more reliable than filament bulbs; they have a longer service life and a much lower current draw. High quality instruments and gauges will be more accurate and reliable than cheaper ones and if you intend to assemble your own loom, do not skimp on wire sizes, connectors or assembly tools.

Positioning the electrical components

Electrical components do not like water, heat or vibration and electronic components can also be sensitive to magnetic fields too unless adequately shielded. In fact a car, particularly the under bonnet area, is a very hostile environment for electrical items in general. Bear this in mind when you are deciding where to position your electrical components. Keep them away, or shield them, from the extreme heat of the exhaust and also the less severe temperatures of the cooling system. Do not position them where water may leak or splash onto them. Any component which is attached to the engine or gearbox unit will

This simple diagram, for a mid engined car, is supplied by Rapidfit so that they can build a custom loom for you. You fill in the dimensions and return it with your order.

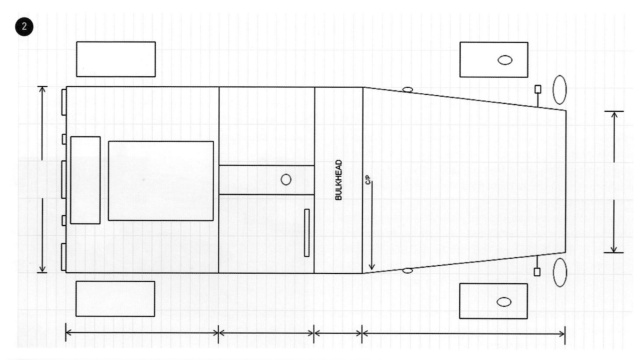

be subject to vibration, and consideration should be given to this when designing the mounting system. Try to avoid mounting the ECU and any of its connecting leads close to the HT leads in order to avoid problems with electromagnetic induction.

The mounting of the battery is very important. The mounting brackets may already be designed into the car, but if not you need to choose a place where it can be securely fastened down by a clamp or a strap. In order to keep the leads short it should be close to the engine and starter motor if possible but other considerations such as space and weight distribution may dictate that it is mounted at the opposite end of the car. If this is the case make sure to use good quality battery cables.

Plan view of my rear-engined Fugitive showing the exact position of the electrical components.

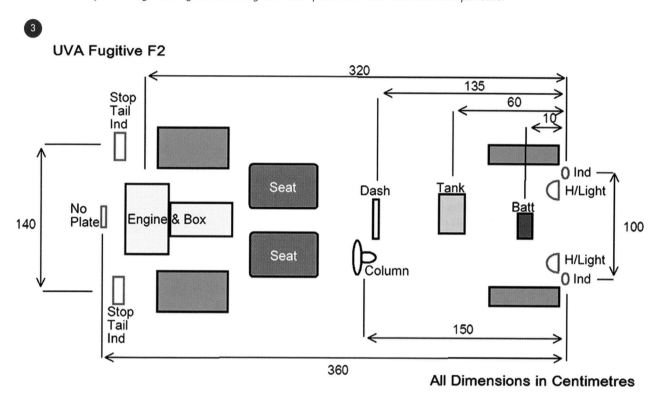

Side elevation of my Fugitive allowing me to plan cable runs and work out the required wire lengths.

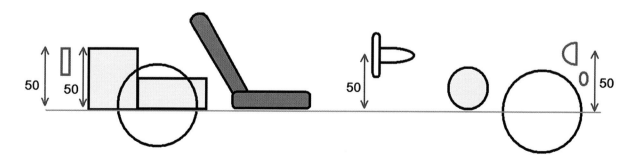

The basic Lucas wiring colours as used in older British cars.

Main	Tracer	Connections
		Earth connections
		Temperature sender to warning light
		Radiator fan power
		Brake lights
		Radiator fan switch
		Headlamp connections
		Main beam
		Dip beam
		Driving lamps
		Main feed from battery (unfused)
		Ignition warning light
		Power to light switch
		Power to horn
		Horn to horn button
		Wiper motor to switch
		Ignition switched power for auxiliary circuits
		Fuel sender
		Temperature gauge to sender
		Reversing lamp
		Left hand indicators
		Right hand indicators
		Brake lights
		Heater
		Heater (high speed)
		Low fuel light
		Voltage stabiliser to instruments
		Screen washer switch to pump
		Indicator switch to flasher unit
		Flasher unit to warning light
		Rear screen washer switch to motor
		Live feeds from battery (fused)
		Fuse to horn relay
		Door switches to interior light
		Side lights and instrument lighting
		Front fog light from switch
		Front fog light power to switch
		Rear fog light from switch
		Rear fog light power to switch
		Instrument lights
		Ignition circuits
		Power to coil positive
		Coil negative to distributor
		Oil pressure sender to warning light
		Radio
		Ignition switch to solenoid

My wiring diagram for the horn and heater circuits on my GTM. The template shows all the components in the car but only those involved in the specific circuit are shown wired up.

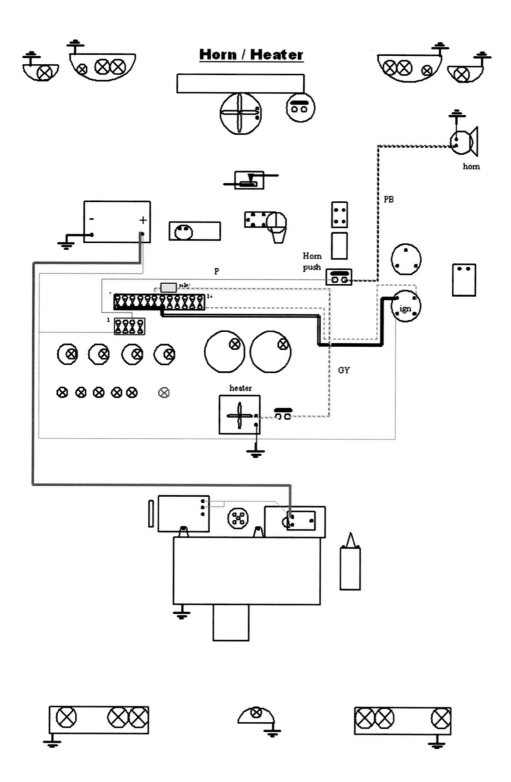

It is also essential to consider cable runs when mounting other components. Wiring looms and connecting leads also need to be kept away or protected from heat and should never be looped across gaps where they could be pulled or snagged. They should be secured to bulkheads or inner wings by 'P' clips or similar at roughly 200mm (8in) intervals. You need to position the components in your car so that these criteria can be met too.

The wiring loom will need to pass through body panels at some point in order to reach the instruments and switches inside the passenger compartment and the rear lights in the boot or rear compartment. The loom must be protected and sealed at these points with suitable grommets and these panel apertures need to be planned into the system. Finally, you need to consider servicing requirements. There is no point in positioning the fuse box or relays in such a way that you have to stand on your head under the dash to simply change a blown fuse. But, on the other hand, corroded fuse or relay terminals due to water ingress is a common cause of electrical failure and can easily be avoided by positioning these components sensibly (Fig 1).

In the early stages of your planning it may help to have a basic outline plan of your car showing the positioning of the major components. This is certainly the route taken by some custom loom manufacturers (Fig 2).

At the time of writing I am in the process of completely rebuilding a UVA Fugitive sand rail which has a rear mounted VW beetle drive train. To aid the planning of my wiring loom I drew out basic diagrams, with dimensions, showing the position of the electrical components (Fig 3/4).

Hopefully these diagrams will enable me to lay out the basic loom quickly with only minor trimming required to tailor it exactly during the fitting process.

Spend time planning the positioning of your electrical components now and you could save a lot of time later on.

Wiring diagrams

If you are rewiring a standard or classic car using an original or replacement harness then you will be able to work from the original wiring diagram as found in the workshop manual. If you are working on a modified, custom or kit car then this may not be an option and you may have to produce your own wiring diagrams. Don't be tempted to make even the slightest wiring modifications without making a permanent record of what you have done. Without this, fault finding will be impossible in the future.

Wiring diagrams can be quite complex to read or draw for a beginner. If you are unsure at first, start with an existing wiring diagram, perhaps from the donor car, modified as required or, if you need to, draw out your own diagram using an existing one as a basis. Use a standard wiring colour code. Lucas (Fig 5) or Ford systems are easy to follow and the correctly coloured wires will be readily available from the retail suppliers.

Trying to include the whole car on one diagram as done by the professionals is tricky. It is easier and clearer to draw out separate diagrams for the lighting, charging and other circuits. When I wired my GTM I used Microsoft Publisher to produce a template. I used this to draw out the individual circuit diagrams (Fig 6).

I also drew detailed schematics for individual components if the wiring was a little complicated (Fig 7). This greatly simplified the job of wiring up the actual component when the time came. The format you use for your wiring diagrams is entirely up to you, but try to make it easy to draw and easy to read. It should be a help in the wiring process, not another chore or hindrance.

Once you are happy with the overall planning of your wiring you are ready to go ahead with the actual process. In the next chapter I will include some sample wiring diagrams for the common vehicle circuits.

The detailed schematic for the wiper motor on my GTM. Note the use of the correct colour codes for the wires.

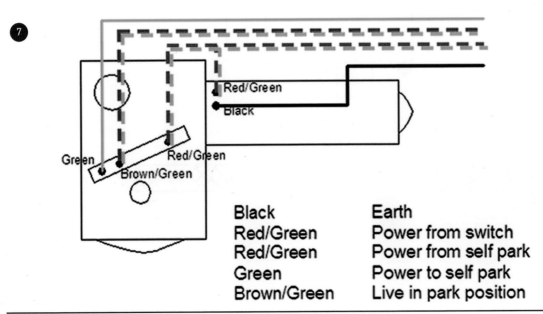

Black — Earth
Red/Green — Power from switch
Red/Green — Power from self park
Green — Power to self park
Brown/Green — Live in park position

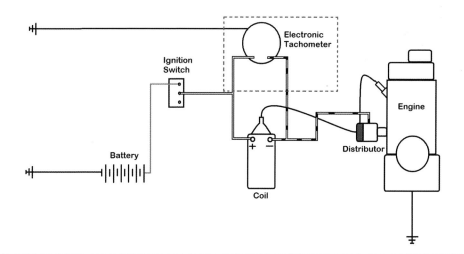

08 Sample Wiring Diagrams

How to wire essential circuits

I **appreciate that**, for many of us, drawing, reading and understanding wiring diagrams are not things which come naturally, so to help clarify these processes I have included a number of sample wiring diagrams for the circuits which are common to most cars.

I have used the Lucas/BSI colour coding, as outlined in Chapter 7 for these diagrams and included an explanation of how each circuit works. Hopefully by the time you have worked your way through a few of these you will begin to understand the general principles and be able to plan and draw your own diagrams for your car. If not, feel free to simply use these diagrams to wire the same systems into your car. If the order of the diagrams seems strange it is because I have tried to arrange them in order of simplicity, so that the basic systems come first and the more complex ones follow later.

Conventions

Although one or two systems are wired directly to the battery and are constantly live, most vehicle circuits are powered from the ignition switch. To avoid confusion in the explanations, I will refer to the switch outputs by their ignition key position.

Position 0 -   Off
Position 1 -   Accessory position live.
Position 2 -   Ignition and auxiliary circuits live. (plus accessories)
Position 3 -   Starter motor live. (plus ignition circuits)

In those circuits where a relay is used, the relay is always drawn in the same orientation and the pin numbers

correspond with this enlarged drawing (Fig 1).

Pins 85 and 86 are connected to the switch and to earth. They can be connected either way round. When the switch is operated a small current flows through the relay coil to energise it. The magnetic field of the coil closes the main relay contacts, switching on the main circuit. These contacts can carry very high currents, normally up to 30A.

Now let's have a look at some real circuits.

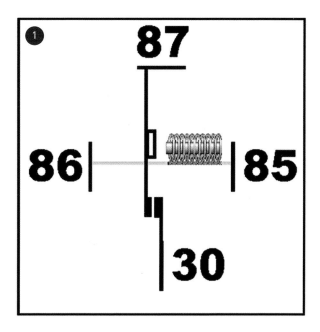

Heater circuit

The heater is an auxiliary circuit and is normally wired so that it works only when the ignition is switched on, so the power is taken from a section of the fuse box wired to Position 2 of the ignition switch. The fuse will protect the circuit should a fault occur. Power then goes to the heater switch. The above circuit assumes that the heater switch is a proper heavy duty unit, so a relay is not included. It also shows a 2-speed heater fan in use. A single speed fan would not need the green/grey wire labelled 'fast'. Depending on how the heater and switch are designed there may be a proper 2-speed motor installed or there may be a single speed motor with a resistor switched in to reduce the speed for the 'slow' setting. Depending on the heater switch setting, power is sent to the heater motor through either the 'slow' or 'fast' circuit, then back to the battery through the earth return.

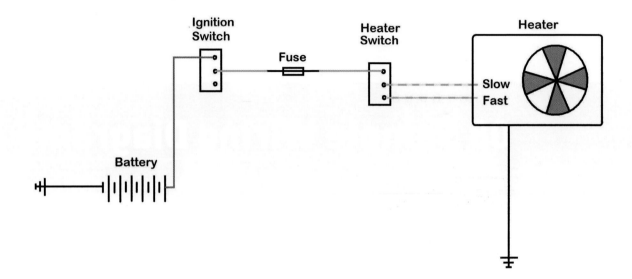

Windscreen wipers

This circuit is very similar to the previous one. Power is taken from a fuse wired to Position 2 of the ignition switch so that the wipers will not run unless the ignition is on. The fuse protects the circuit in the event of a fault. The power then goes to the windscreen wiper switch. This circuit shows the now IVA mandatory 2-speed wiper system and once again assumes that the switch is a dedicated unit capable of carrying the required current without the use of a relay. The switch sends the power to either the low or high speed circuits depending on its setting. Wipers need to be able to self-park after they are switched off so an independent live feed is sent to the 'Park' circuit, regardless of the position of the wiper switch. The earth return completes the circuit back to the battery.

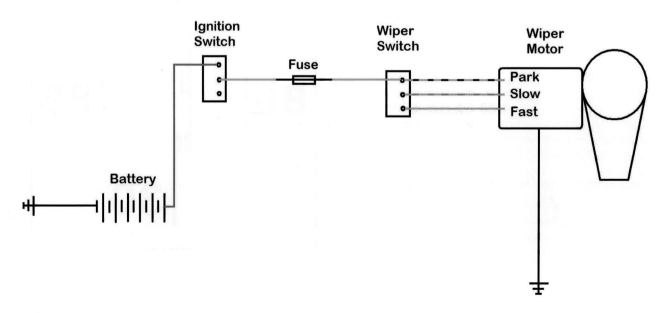

Ignition system

This circuit applies to those vehicles using conventional contact breakers or 'points'. Electronic systems or engine management systems have control boxes which are integrated into the engine sensors, but the unit would still take its power from the same source.

Obviously this system is also powered from Position 2 of the ignition switch, but is often not fused. The power supply from the switch is connected to the + or SW connection on the ignition coil. The – or CB terminal of the coil is connected to the contact breakers and condenser in the distributor. The circuit is completed by the earth return through the distributor body, the engine casings and the engine earthing strap. When the points open, the coil generates a high voltage pulse which is sent to the distributor cap, the rotor arm and finally the spark plug.

If an electronic tachometer is fitted, it will normally have three connections. Power is taken from the + side of the coil, ignition pulses are detected at the – coil connection and the unit will be earthed to complete the circuit.

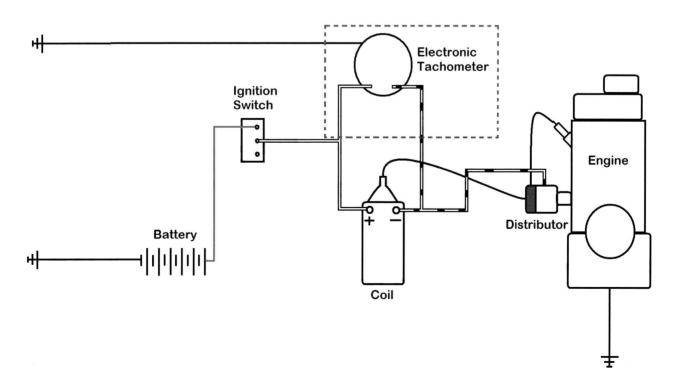

Starting and charging system

Starting – When the ignition switch is turned to Position 3, power flows to the solenoid to energise it. The solenoid connects the heavy duty power lead from the battery directly to the starter motor causing it to spin. If the solenoid and the starter motor form a combined unit, they are both earthed through the engine and its earthing strap. On older cars the solenoid may be mounted separately, in which case it will need its own earth return.

Charging – This diagram shows the charging circuit for an alternator system. A dynamo circuit is more complex as it uses an external regulator unit.

When the ignition switch is turned to Position 2 power flows through the warning light bulb and energises the field coils in the alternator. This is necessary so that it can begin to produce power. When the engine is running the alternator generates current which is fed to the battery though the heavy brown wire and to the field coils internally to keep them energised. The ignition light goes out. If the alternator stops charging for any reason, the warning light will switch on again.

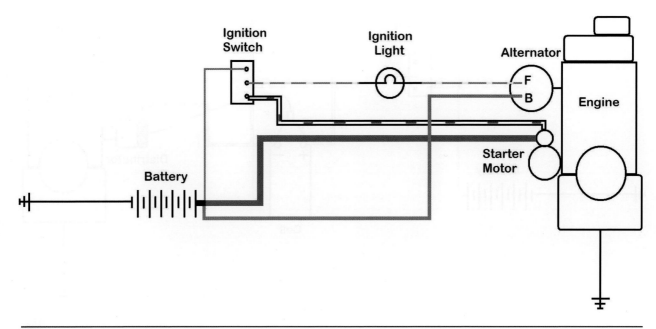

Brake lights

The brake light circuit does not need to work unless the ignition is switched on, so once again it takes its power from a fuse connected to Position 2 of the ignition switch. The brake light switch may be a mechanical unit operated directly from the brake pedal or a hydraulic unit plumbed into a convenient brake line. Either way, all that is needed is a simple SPST momentary switch. When the switch is operated power flows to the brake light bulbs or to the brake light filaments in twin filament stop/tail light bulbs. Twin filament bulbs are normally 5w/21w with the more powerful filament being the brake light. If you wanted to fit a third high level brake light you would simply connect it to the output of the switch in parallel with the other two.

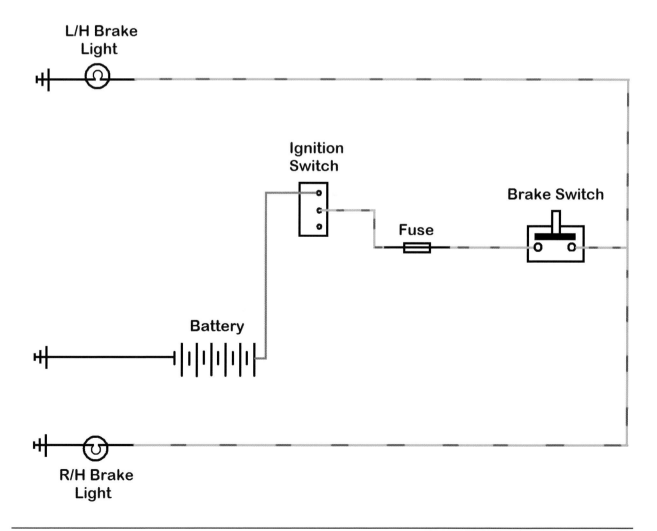

Radiator fan

An electric radiator fan can be wired to operate only with the ignition switched on by powering it from Position 2 on the ignition switch, but in my cars I prefer to wire it to a source which is constantly live so that it will continue to operate even after the engine is switched off. Once the coolant temperature falls below the preset level the thermostatic switch will turn the fan off anyway.

This circuit uses a relay to reduce the current passing through the thermostatic switch. The power is taken from a fuse which is wired directly to the battery so that it is permanently live. It is essential that all permanently live power feeds are fused, as there is no way to switch them off if a fault occurs. The power is taken to the relay and also to the thermostatic switch which is mounted in a hose or the radiator so that it can sense the coolant temperature. When the coolant reaches the preset temperature the switch contacts close. A small current flows to earth through the relay coil. This causes the main relay contacts to close, allowing a high current to flow to the radiator fan. When the coolant temperature falls, the switch opens and the relay turns the fan off again.

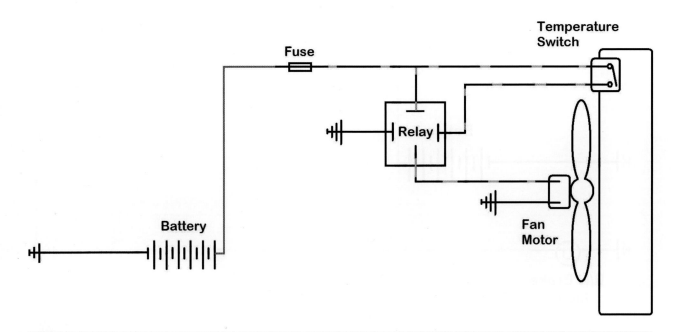

Horn

There are two ways of wiring a horn. When horn buttons were mounted in the centre of the steering wheel, horns were wired to be permanently live and were earthed through the horn button to operate them. Later cars with stalk mounted horn buttons use horns which are permanently earthed through their mounting brackets or separate wires and are supplied with a live feed to operate them when the button is pressed.

Horn (permanent live)

Once again a relay is used to reduce the current passing through the switch. In this circuit the horn is permanently connected to a fused constant live supply but it could be powered from Position 2 of the ignition switch if you wish. When the horn button is pressed a small current flows to earth through the relay coil. This energises the relay and closes the main contacts. This connects the horn, which is already live, to the earth return, allowing current to flow.

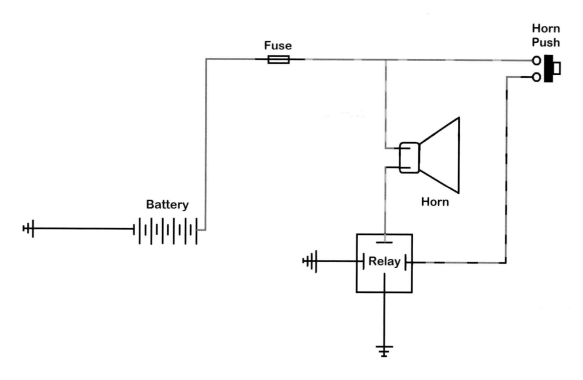

Horn (permanent earth)

Power is supplied from a fused constant live supply but could be taken from Position 2 of the ignition switch if you wish. When the horn button is pressed a small current flows to earth through the relay coil. This energises the relay and closes the main contacts, supplying the power needed to sound the horn.

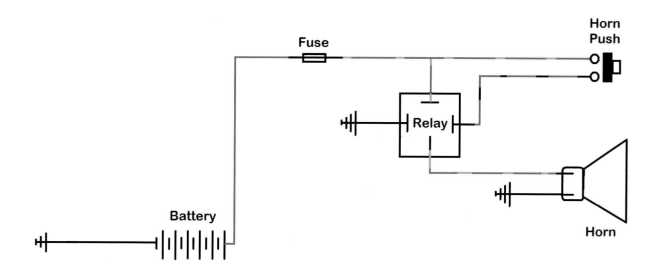

Instruments

This circuit shows how to wire in the four gauges which I consider to be essential and always fit to my cars. If you are using mechanical temperature and oil pressure gauges they are operated by capillary sender units and need no wiring apart from the internal illumination. This diagram shows the wiring for the electronic versions of the gauges.

The power is taken from a fuse connected to Position 2 on the ignition switch, so the gauges will only operate when the ignition is switched on. I have shown a voltage stabiliser in the circuit, but not all gauges require this, so it may not be necessary. The instructions supplied with the gauge will tell you this. The fuel gauge, temperature gauge and oil pressure gauge are all wired in the same way. One terminal is connected to the power supply and the other is connected to the matching sender unit. The voltmeter (or battery condition meter) needs no sender unit. It simply needs a Position 2 live supply at one terminal and the other is connected to earth. Never connect a voltmeter to a voltage stabiliser unit. It needs to measure the full battery or alternator voltage.

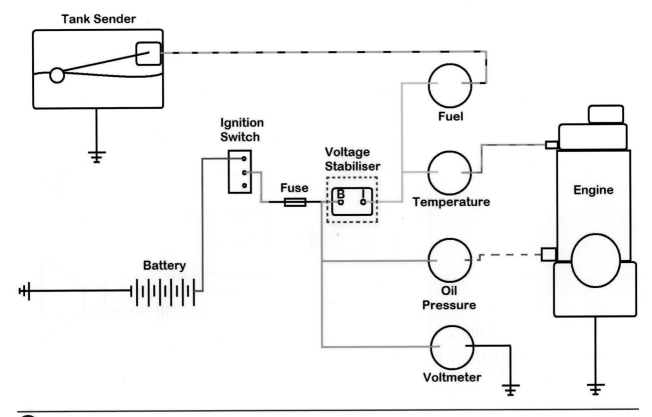

Indicators

The indicators take their power from a fused Position 2 supply, so they will only work when the ignition is on. From the fuse the power goes straight to the flasher unit. I have shown a two-terminal flasher on this diagram. Three-terminal units normally have a separate earth connection. The power then goes to the indicator switch. This is 'off' in the centre position but connects either to the L/H or R/H circuits when moved appropriately. All the bulbs within a circuit are arranged in parallel, so if one bulb blows the rest continue to work, but the flash rate changes since less current is now flowing through the flasher unit. This is a deliberate feature to warn the driver of the bulb failure.

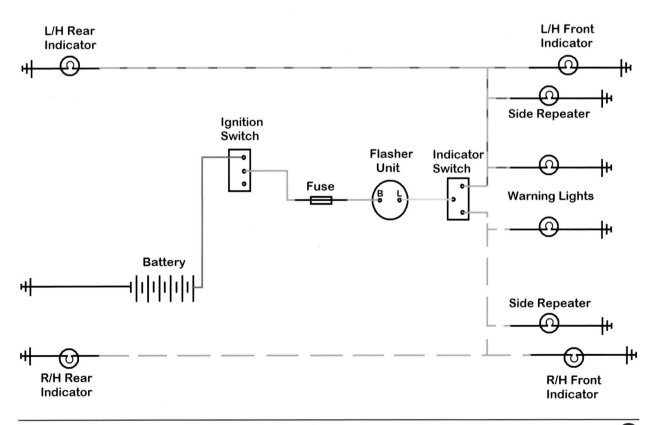

Lights

There are two separate power supplies in use here. The main light switch is powered directly from the battery so that the side and rear lights can be left on as parking lights even with the ignition off and the car locked. The headlight relays are powered from Position 2 on the ignition switch, so the headlights will only work when the ignition is on. I have used separate fused supplies and separate relays for the main and dip beam circuits. This is an additional safety feature.

With the light switch moved to Position 1, power flows along the red wire to the fuse box. The fused supply then powers the side lights, instrument lights and rear lights.

When the light switch is moved to Position 2 the side light circuit stays connected but power also flows along the blue wire to the dip switch. There is no 'off' position on the dip switch. It simply directs power to one circuit or the other. In the 'dip' position a small current travels along the blue/red cable to the appropriate relay, where it energises the coil to close the main contacts. This switches on the main power supply to the headlight dip beam filaments. This power comes from the ignition switch via the fuse box. When the dip switch is moved to the 'main' position the same sequence occurs in the main beam circuit.

Obviously I have not drawn a diagram for every circuit in a motor vehicle. Nor is it possible for me to draw circuit diagrams for specific components or accessories. The purpose of this chapter is simply to introduce you to the way in which circuits are represented and to hopefully give you enough background knowledge to be able to plan and draw your own circuits before you wire them.

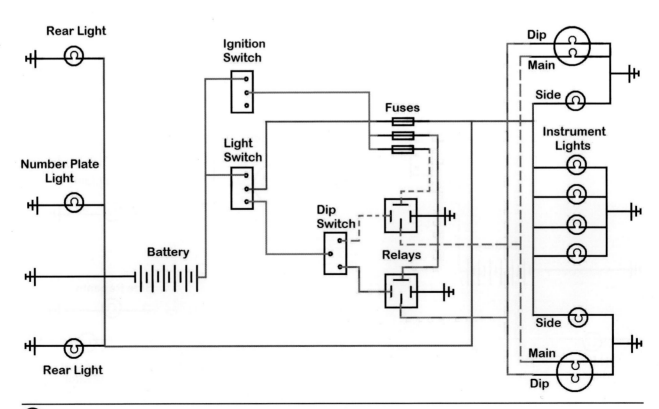

09 Fuse Box

Planning and wiring

Once you have decided which electrical systems and components you will be fitting to your car, you are in a position to be able to start planning out the wiring. Personally I always start with the fuse box. This is effectively the central hub of your vehicle's electrical system. Power is fed to it directly from the battery or the ignition switch, and the fuse box then distributes fused power supplies to the individual circuits or systems around the car.

In the chapter dealing with power supplies I briefly mentioned that modern cars protect their circuits with far more fuses than was common 40 years ago. This is partly due to the fact that modern cars have far more electrical systems than they did in the past and partly because it is now common practice to sub-divide systems and to fuse individual components. For example a modern car will often have separate fuses for nearside and offside headlamps, so that in the event of a failure only one headlight will be lost.

The number of fuses you use is entirely up to you. You can

choose to use fewer fuses by leaving some systems unprotected, but this is dangerous and is not an option I would recommend. You can reduce the number of fuses by allowing different systems to share each fuse, but if you are unfortunate enough to blow a fuse at any time you will lose all the systems connected to it. Neither of these options is particularly desirable, although they used to be common practice on older cars. The early Minis, for example, only had two fuses. One fuse protected the horn and interior light and the second protected the indicators, brake lights and instruments. All the other circuits, including the ignition and main lighting systems, were completely unprotected. I once had a wiring harness burn out in my Mini when the control box cut-out failed to disconnect the battery from the dynamo after I had switched off the ignition.

A selection of fuse boxes for blade type fuses. The two units at the lower left connect from the side, the rest from the rear.

Obviously, the number of fuses you use will depend on what systems or components you are wiring into your car. I would suggest that, as a minimum, the following circuits need to be fused.			
Main beam (Better to fuse each side separately)	30A	**Brake lights**	10A
Dip beam (Better to fuse each side separately)	30A	**Side lights**	10A
		Rear lights (Better to fuse each side separately)	10A
Radiator fan	30A	**Horn**	10A
Wash/wipe	20A	**Accessories/radio**	10A
Heater motor	15A		

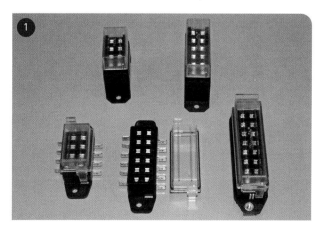

These are modular units. They will clip together as required. On the left is the 4 way relay box, on the right is the 16 way fuse box.

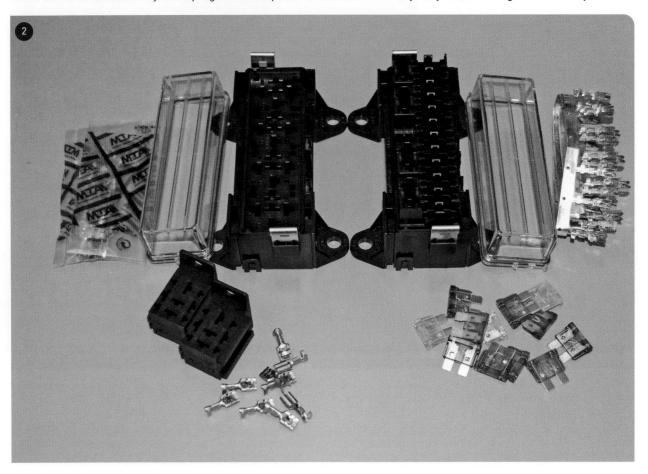

Ignition systems were not normally fused on earlier cars but on modern vehicles equipped with ECUs it may be advisable to do so.

Obviously if you have other electrical accessories such as electric windows or central locking, they should also be protected with a suitable fuse.

If you follow my recommendations you will be looking at around 10 to 15 individual fuses. It is perfectly possible to wire them into their circuits using a separate in-line fuse holder in each circuit, but this would be untidy, inefficient and would make fault finding more difficult. It is far better and easier in the long term to use a single fixed fuse box capable of holding the required number of fuses (Fig 1).

Some of the units available are modular and can be clipped together along with relay boxes to form a complete power supply unit. They are all capable of being panel mounted and have connectors which can be accessed either from the side or from the rear of the box. If possible, choose a fuse box with a lid and protected terminals (Fig 2).

Supplying the power

Most of the systems in a car take their power from the ignition switch. They will not operate unless the ignition is switched to the 'run' position. The headlights, wipers, heater and obviously the ignition itself are wired in this way. Car audio equipment is also normally powered from the ignition switch but operates with the key in the 'accessories' position rather than the full 'on' position.

Some electrical systems need to take their power directly from the battery so that they can be operated at any time without the ignition being switched on. These include side and rear lights (for parking), hazard warning flashers, security devices and possibly the radiator cooling fan. If it is wired in this way it will continue to run after the engine is switched off to help dissipate residual heat. In view of this, you need to arrange for three separate power supplies to your fuse box (or possibly three separate fuse boxes) so that you can power the car systems appropriately.

As a guide these are the systems which I think should be powered by each of the three different supplies.

Ignition live
Ignition
Indicators
Brake lights
Main beam
Dip beam
Fog lights
Wash/Wipe
Heater
Instruments

This is the schematic which I drew for my GTM fuse box complete with colour coded wiring and fuse values. It made actually assembling the unit so much easier.

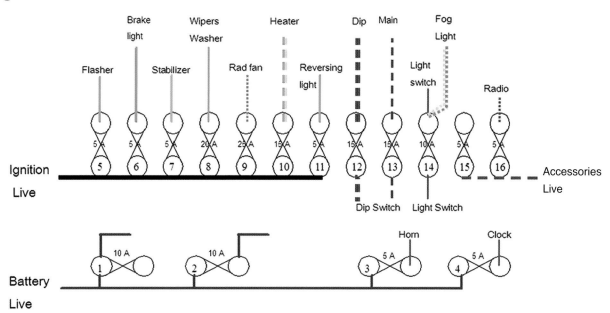

Accessory live
    Radio/CD/mp3
    Power socket (or permanent live)

Permanent live
    Radiator fan
    Side lights
    Horn
    Hazard Flashers
    Clock
    Power socket (or accessory live)

Note that some ignition switches disconnect the 'accessory' position internally when the starter motor is energised in order to reduce the load on the battery. Bear this in mind when you are choosing the power source for your accessories.

Once you have decided how you will fuse your electrical system and what hardware you will use, you are in a position to be able to plan out the details of your fusebox. The format you use is not important. It is meant to make the wiring process easier, so use whatever system is clearest for you. This is the diagram I drew for my GTM fuse box using Microsoft Publisher (Fig 3).

The layout and colour coding on the diagram is the same as the actual component so that I could follow it easily. You will see that the three power supplies have their own separate areas within the fuse box and that there are some unused fuses (1, 2 and 15) which I provided to allow me to safely add components in the future should it prove necessary. The wires which carry the power supplies to the fuse box must be capable of carrying a high current. Make

The fuse box and relay box were clipped together to form a single power supply unit with multi-plugs to easily connect the separate systems.

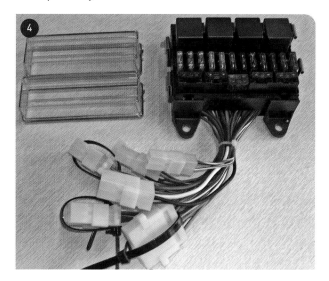

sure they have sufficient capacity.

The actual component I used was of the modular type which enabled me to attach a relay box too. The finished article was quite a neat unit (Fig 4).

I used multi-plugs to allow the fuse box to be wired separately then mounted and connected to the sections of the loom as needed.

A relatively recent development, which simplifies the planning process greatly, is the CBS Wiring Module produced by Car Builder Solutions (Fig 5).

This module contains the fuse box, the hazard and

indicator flasher units and relays for the horn and radiator fan. They are pre-wired to a connector block which enables it to be quickly connected to the rest of the car wiring. Obviously, as a commercial unit, it may not contain exactly the same circuits as your ideal design but it is certainly a good starting point.

If you get the fuse box right, it will make wiring the rest of the car so much easier. Don't be afraid to spend time planning this unit. It will be time well spent.

The CBS Wiring Module combines the fuse box, flasher units and some relays in a pre-wired module which greatly simplifies the wiring process.

5

10 Making A Custom Wiring Loom

The ultimate DIY answer

If you have read the chapter on planning you should, by now, have decided which components and systems you are fitting, where they will be located within the vehicle and how you will route and retain the harness to connect them up. You should also have decided on a colour code for your harness and drawn out basic wiring diagrams for each system.

The first step in assembling the harness is to measure up and buy the necessary wires and components. Using your outline plan of your vehicle or the actual vehicle itself, work out or measure the length of each of the individual wires you will need to assemble your harness. Allow at least 10% extra length on each wire in case you need to do some minor re-routing during the assembly. Make sure that the wire grades you purchase are correct for the loads they will need to carry. Buy the terminals, connectors and multiplugs which you have designed into your system along with the correct crimping tools and suitable wire strippers. Finally make sure that you buy all the ancillary components such as fuse boxes, relays, grommets etc. It is frustrating to have to stop work on a job because a minor component has been forgotten.

Components such as the fuse box, relay box, dashboard and steering column are easier to wire off the car. If they are wired as separate units and connected through multi-plugs, they can be quickly disconnected from the loom and removed from the vehicle for easy maintenance (Fig 1).

The actual process of making the harness is best done on the vehicle itself. Try to work in an organised manner and fully complete each module before moving on to the next. Within each module, I wire the individual circuits one at a time and, if possible, test them too.

The process is best illustrated by a real example. My GTM had a removable flip front (Fig 2) so the front harness module

This is the dash panel from my GTM wired as a separate module. Even with a mechanical speedo and a capillary oil pressure gauge it could be removed from the car in around 10 minutes.

The whole bonnet section lifts off so the wiring for that section has to be quickly detachable too.

These wire bag ties work very well as temporary wraps while you are assembling the loom.

This is the temporary loom secured with small cable ties. The kitchen floor was the only sensible place to lay out the loom.

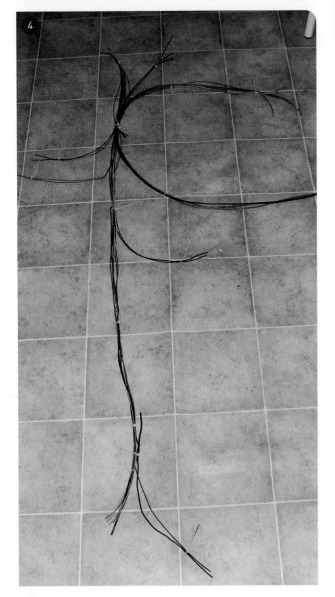

This is the fixed section of the front loom fully completed. In the foreground is the section leading to the lights.

needed to be in two sections. One section, which was fixed to the car, took power to the horn, wiper, washer pump, brake light switch and radiator fan. The removable section continued the power feed to the lights and indicators on the bonnet.

To assemble the loom, each individual wire was laid in position on the car and trimmed roughly to length allowing a little extra to attach the connectors. Where possible I normally start with the longer wires. As the rest of the wires were added they were temporarily clipped together using releasable cable ties, bag ties or masking tape (Fig 3).

When all the wires were temporarily held in position the loom was removed from the car (Fig 4). The temporary ties were replaced with permanent fixings. I used small cable ties but insulating tape or self amalgamating tape would have been fine too.

If you are using PVC sleeving, braided sleeving or solid convoluted tubing to wrap the harness, it needs to be fitted at this stage. It cannot be fitted after the connectors are in place. Split trunking or spiral wrap can be fitted later if you wish.

With the sleeving fitted, the harness can be put back into the car so that the individual wires can be trimmed to their final length and the connectors and plugs can be fitted (Fig 5).

The removable part of the harness was also produced on

This is the front module fitted into the car. The rear section goes through the bulkhead to connect to the dashboard and steering column.

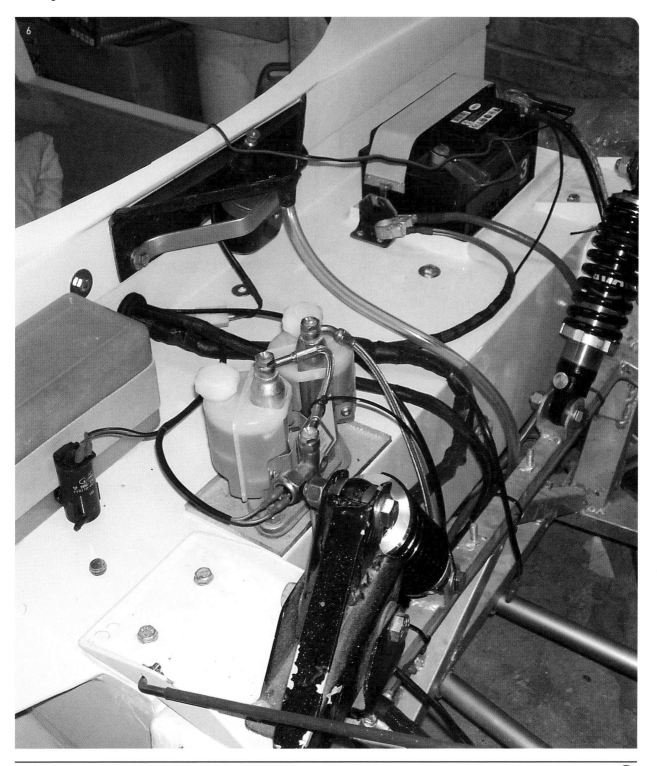

The front end of the loom connects to the horn and radiator fan. The multi-plug connects to the removable part of the harness powering the front lights.

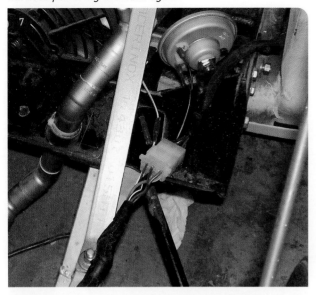

This is the removable section of the front loom. On the right is the main connector.

The wiring to the lights is sealed with PVC sleeving. The inner wings have grommets fitted to seal the cable access holes and the connectors are located on the other side of the inner wings for protection.

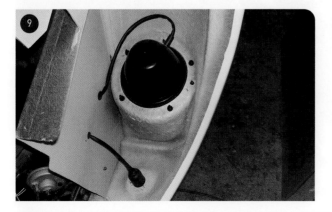

the car in the same way then removed for finishing (Fig 8).

My car was intended to be my daily all weather transport, so I designed the loom to be as reliable as possible. All the connection points were protected from water ingress by locating them in protected areas (Fig 9). I would have done this even if I had been using waterproof plugs and sockets.

This is a section of the engine loom which connects to the distributor, the coil and the solenoid. The main engine loom runs along the upper chassis rail.

The copper pipes are the radiator and heater plumbing and the black plastic pipes are the conduits for the wiring and control cables.

A selection of bases and ties which are securely fixed by screws or rivets.

You can't be too careful with water and electrics.

Using this method, each section or module of the loom can be built up individually then connected together to form the complete wiring harness (Fig 10).

If no removable panels are needed it is possible to make the harness in one single piece, and it could be argued that by eliminating plugs and connectors the reliability will be improved and any small voltage drops across connections will be eliminated. The disadvantages are mostly concerned with the handling and fitting of a one-piece loom. The whole length of the wiring harness would have to be fed in and out of the car during each stage of assembly and fitting.

Final fitting

During the course of construction, your new wiring loom will have been trial fitted to the vehicle a number of times but never fully secured. When you are sure that all the required fabrication has taken place you need to secure the loom into the vehicle using suitable permanent fixings. The mounting points should have been established at an early stage in the planning and should have taken account of the current regulations. At the time of writing, the IVA regulations for

vehicle wiring state 'all electrical cables/wires must be free from chaffing and secured at intervals of at least every 300mm unless contained in a secure hollow component.'

The 'hollow component' referred to could be a conduit or a hollow body or chassis member. When I assembled the chassis of my Coupe, I built the plumbing and electrical conduits in at a very early stage (Fig 11).

There are a number of ways of securing the wiring harness as it runs along body panels. Cable ties can be used if they are secured using a proper base. Personally I would not rely on the self-adhesive type to last very long. I would always use the screw fixing bases (Fig 12).

My own preference is to use 'P' clips in either plastic (normally nylon) or rubber lined metal to secure a wiring loom. They are available in a number of sizes.

Whichever system you choose, make sure that the harness is firmly secured and well away from moving parts, heat and water ingress. Make sure none of the connections to any of the components are under strain or tension and do not drape wires over areas where they may be snagged during routine servicing of the vehicle. Have a look at a few examples of production car wiring and you will quickly get the idea.

A selection of Nylon 'P' clips. If you use pop rivets to secure these make sure you use a washer to prevent the rivet pulling through

These are rubber lined aluminium 'P' clips but they are also available in galvanised steel too. The rubber lining is essential to prevent chafing of the wiring.

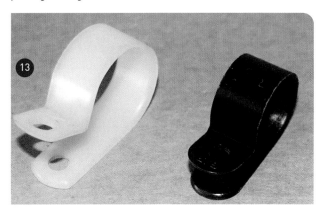

11 Attaching Connectors

Crimping and soldering

A decision you have to make at a fairly early stage is whether you want to solder or crimp your connectors onto the wires. Both methods need some specialist equipment and both need some skill and practice. In practical terms a good crimped connection is as electrically sound and secure as a good soldered connection. On the other hand, a poor soldered connection can be every bit as bad as a poor crimped connection.

Basics: Wire stripping

No matter how minor the wiring job you intend to do, you will not get far before you find that you need to remove the insulation from a wire. In an emergency I have been known to use my teeth, but I cannot recommend it. I have also seen scissors and Stanley knives used, but I prefer to keep all my fingers and thumbs attached thank you. A basic set of wire strippers (Fig 1)

Automatic wire strippers. They are self-adjusting for a wide range of wire gauges.

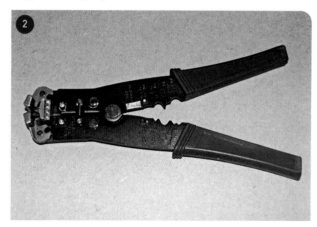

Basic wire strippers. You set the wire thickness by moving the adjusting screw in the slot.

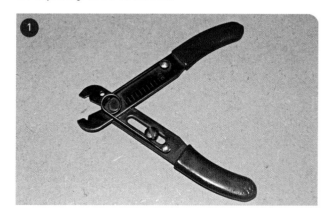

The jaws are double acting. They move up to grip the wire then move apart to strip off the covering.

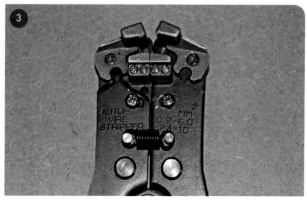

The first stage. The wire is gripped ready to strip.

The second stage. The jaws have moved apart and stripped off the required length of insulation.

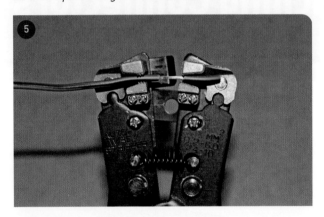

is so cheap that you should really have a pair around the house, just like electrician's screwdrivers and torches.

If you own or intend to buy a crimping tool for your project, then it will already have wire strippers built in.

If you are completely rewiring your car or making extensive modifications, then you might think about investing in some automatic wire strippers (Fig 2). They can handle almost any thickness of wire without any adjustments. The jaws of the tool are normally sprung open and are serrated to grip the insulation (Fig 3).

The wire is placed into the jaws and the handles are squeezed. The jaws automatically move upwards to close on the wire and grip it firmly (Fig 4). When the handles are squeezed fully, the jaws move apart and strip off the insulation (Fig 5).

The process is very quick and this tool, though more expensive, is ideal if you have a lot of wiring to do.

Soldering connectors

To solder successfully the wire and terminal must both get hot enough to melt the solder so that it flows into the joint by capillary action. Copper conducts heat away quickly, so a small soldering iron is no use at all... the components will not reach the required temperature. I would suggest an iron with a minimum power rating of 50w and 100w would be better. I use a gas-powered soldering iron for wires over 2.5mm^2 and for battery terminals I use a small blowlamp.

The components must be clean and free from grease, oil or oxidation. Flux is used in soldering to remove or prevent oxidation on the hot metal. Most solder available now will be flux cored and should need no extra flux, but personally I

These are the tools I use for general soldering. The iron is 75w, the solder is flux cored but I also have a flux pen and flux paste.

have always produced better soldered joints using separate flux too (Fig 6).

If you are starting with a new soldering iron it needs to be 'tinned'. Allow the iron to reach full heat then wipe it on a damp sponge or tissue to clean it. Dip it in the flux if you have any. Immediately melt a small amount of solder onto the working area of the tip. It should flow over the clean area producing a thin even coating. The iron is now ready for use.

Plug the iron in and leave it to heat up fully. Wipe the tip on a damp sponge or tissue then dip it into the flux. The flux is normally acid based and as it boils it cleans off any oxidation (Fig 7). Don't breathe in the fumes.

To be sure the solder has penetrated the joint fully I 'tin' both components separately then fuse them together. I normally 'tin' the wire first. The insulation is stripped off to leave about 6mm of bare wire. This is then dipped into the flux so that it will be cleaned when the iron is applied (Fig 8).

You need some way of holding the components still whilst they are soldered. I have a small hobby vice which, like most of my tools, is well used. The solder and the iron are held onto the wire until the solder melts and completely wets the wire (Fig 9).

Try not to let the solder penetrate beyond the insulation.

The hot soldering iron oxidises quickly. The boiling flux removes the oxidation.

The bare wire is dipped in the flux to form a thin coating which will clean the wire during the process.

This is where the problem with embrittlement can occur. Remove the heat and allow the wire to cool (Fig 10).

The same process is used to 'tin' the terminal. Use a match or toothpick to put a small amount of flux into the terminal then hold it firmly and melt some solder into the joint area (Fig 11).

Once again, when cool, the solder should have a smooth shiny silver appearance (Fig 12). Leave it to cool before you

Apply just enough heat to 'tin' the wire.

The solder should have a smooth shiny silver appearance.

A little more heat may be needed here. Make sure the solder flows easily.

touch it. 200deg C is hot!

Hold the two components together and heat them until the solder melts and flows together. Do not move them as the solder cools... you will get a 'dry' joint which is weak and a poor conductor (Fig 13).

The finished joint should be shiny and silver (Fig 14). If it has a rough or crystalline appearance it is a 'dry' joint and you will have to re-melt it. Try to get it right first time, as repeated heating and cooling will damage the wire and the insulation.

If the terminal has crimp tabs on it, then fold them over to support the joint and to secure the insulation. If you have overheated the wire, the insulation may have melted back away from the terminal. Heat shrink tubing can be used to solve this problem but you have to remember to slide it on before you solder the second terminal on the wire (Fig 15).

The finished joint. Fold over the tabs to hold the insulation and support the joint.

Heat shrink tubing can be used to tidy up the joint and add additional protection against breakage.

Try to keep the solder away from the area of the insulation clip.

Rest your hand on something solid so that you can hold the wire still as it cools.

Using crimp connectors

Pre-insulated terminals are readily available and are quick and easy to use. No separate insulation sleeve is required. The non-insulated variety take just a little more work but, in my opinion, look more professional and are certainly more compact (Fig 16). They can also be used in multi-connectors too. The two types use different crimping tools but both tools are cheap and readily available.

The crimping tools are available at various prices. Mine are the cheaper versions but are still perfectly capable of producing good sound connections (Fig 17). Make sure you buy the correct tool for the type of terminals you will be using.

The different coloured terminals are for different wire sizes.

Red	0.65 - 1.50 mm2
Blue	1.50 – 2.50 mm2
Yellow	2.50 – 6.00 mm2

Be aware that the actual terminals are different sizes too. A blue bullet will not fit into a red socket for example.

On the left are the pre-insulated terminals. The other types, on the right, need the separate insulating covers shown.

My well used crimping tools. Get the correct one for the terminals you will be using.

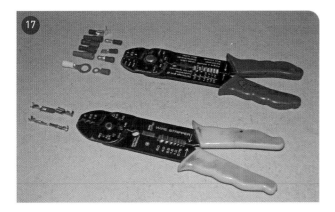

The crimping jaws are colour coded to match the terminals.

The strands will spread unless they are twisted together.

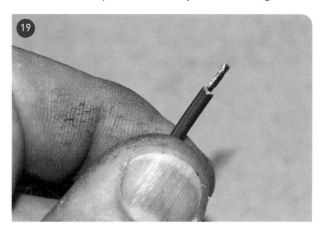

The insulation is pushed fully home and the wire is just visible beyond the insulation.

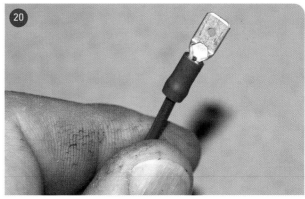

The correct position for the terminal before crimping begins.

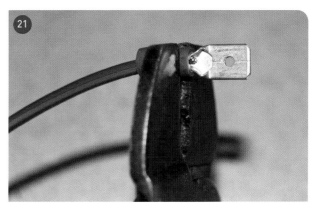

This is a correctly formed wiring crimp.

This is the correct position for the tool when crimping the insulation only.

This is the completed terminal with a correctly formed insulation crimp.

The tool used to crimp pre-insulated terminals has three different crimping jaws. They are colour coded to match the terminals used (Fig 18).

The first step is to strip back the insulation to produce about 6mm of bare wire. The strands then need twisting together slightly to stop them spreading as they are pushed into the terminal (Fig 19).

The wire is then pushed into the terminal until the insulation butts up against the stop (Fig 20). The wire should not protrude too far out of the crimp area or it can prevent

the terminals linking correctly.

The terminal is then gripped firmly in the jaws of the crimping tool so that the split in the metal terminal is facing one of the jaws (Fig 21).

The handles of the tool are then squeezed hard to crimp the terminal. Both the metal conductor and the plastic covering are crimped onto the wire together (Fig 22).

Using the same jaws, the tool is used to grip the terminal again but this time only the plastic insulation is to be

This crimping tool is used for non-insulated terminals.

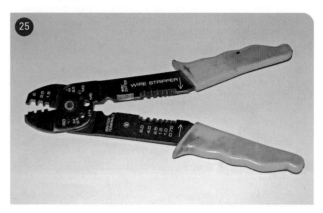

The jaws are different on each side of the tool so it must be lined up correctly in use.

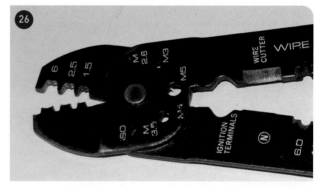

If you want to use an insulating sleeve slide it on before you start.

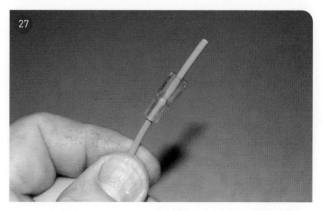

crimped so the tool is moved down to about 1mm from the end of the plastic (Fig 23).

The tool is squeezed gently this time. There is no metal in this area, only plastic, and it will crack if too much force is used (Fig 24). The insulation crimp is important. It supports the wire and stops it flexing in use.

If you do this correctly the wire should not pull out of the terminal even with moderate force. If it does you need to do

About 6mm of bare wire with the strands twisted together so they don't fray.

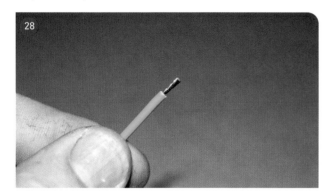

The ends of the insulation crimp may need a gentle squeeze.

The terminal is held gently in the largest jaws. Get it the right way round.

it again. The whole process, with practice, takes about 10 seconds for each terminal.

If you choose to use non-insulated terminals, the method of crimping is basically the same but a little trickier at first due to the design of the hardware. The crimping tool looks similar at first glance but the jaws are different (Fig 25). They are not symmetrical. One side forms a support or 'anvil' for the terminal and the other side is shaped to form the crimp (Fig 26). This means the terminal must be placed in the jaws

This is how it looks from the other side of the tool.

With the wire held in place gently squeeze the tool as far as it will go.

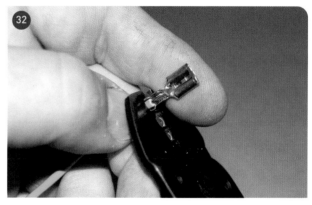

The sides should fold over nicely and bite into the insulation.

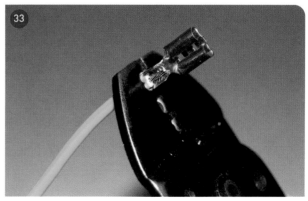

in the correct orientation.

If you intend using the terminals in a multi-plug then no insulation is needed but if the terminal will be exposed then you need to fit a separate sleeve. Slide this on before you begin the crimping process (Fig 27).

Strip off about 6mm of insulation and twist the exposed strands together gently to stop them fraying when you are working with the wire (Fig 28).

Check to see that the sides of the terminal will fit in the jaws of the tool. They occasionally need squeezing together a little before use (Fig 29).

I find it easier to crimp the insulation first with this type of terminal. Carefully place the insulation area of the terminal

into the tool. I use the larger jaws for this part of the process. Line it up as shown in the illustration (Fig 30/31). Grip it gently and don't crimp it yet!

Place the wire into the terminal and hold it in position. There is no stop this time, so you will have to line it up by eye. Check the illustration to see the correct position. When everything is lined up correctly squeeze the handles of the tool slowly until they stop moving (Fig 32). You cannot overdo this as they close completely when the crimp is correct.

The sides of the terminal should fold over nicely then bite into the insulation to give a secure hold on the wire (Fig 33).

The crimp should be smooth and symmetrical and the

This is what the insulation crimp should look like.

This is the completed crimp. This is what you should be able to produce with a hand tool like this.

For the wire crimp a smaller set of jaws are used. Once again make sure you have it the right way round.

The insulating sleeve can be slid into place.

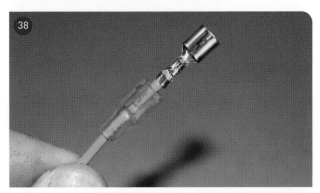

The sides of the terminal fold over and crimp the conductor.

The completed terminal.

wire should be held securely in the terminal (Fig 34).

If you are happy with the result then you can move on to the second step. Grip the conductor area of the terminal in the middle sized jaws of the tool (Fig 35). Make sure you have it the correct way round or you will have wasted all your careful work so far.

Squeeze the tool to crimp the terminal onto the wire. Once again, you can squeeze hard as the jaws will close fully when the crimp is complete (Fig 36). The sides of the terminal should fold over and grip the copper wire firmly.

With a little practice you will be able to produce good quality crimps like this (Fig 37). They will never look quite as

neat as a machine produced crimp but will be just as efficient in use.

Once the crimp is completed you can slide the insulating sleeve into position if required (Fig 38). It is a good idea to fill the sleeve with Vaseline or silicone grease at this stage to prevent corrosion in the future.

As I said at the start of this section, these terminals are slightly trickier to use but once you have tried a few you will have no problem producing good secure crimps (Fig 39). Personally I prefer these terminals. I think that they look more professional than the pre-insulated ones and the insulation crimp is certainly more secure. They are also cheaper. If you want to use multi-plugs then you will have to use this type of terminal anyway.

Multiplugs

Multiplugs are easy to use and have been designed for quick and easy assembly. The simplest type uses the normal 6mm male and female blade connectors. In order to locate the connectors securely in the plug or socket, they have small tags which lock into moulded slots in the plastic body (Fig 40).

The connectors themselves can be crimped or soldered onto the wire as previously described (Fig 41).

The multiplug body has moulded slots for the connectors

6mm male and female blade connectors. The locating tag is clearly visible on the male blade (top).

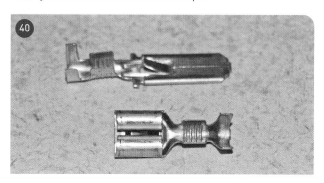

The female blade connector crimped onto the wire as described earlier. The locating tag can be seen on this female blade.

A close up of the plastic receptacle showing the slots for the locating tags.

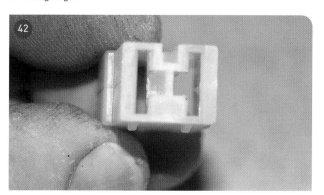

The connector slides into the terminal block and locks securely into place.

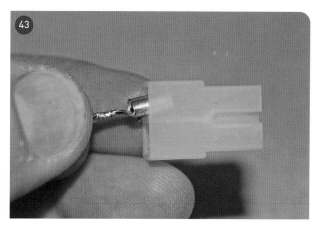

This is the female blade correctly fitted into the 2-way plug body. It cannot be pulled out unless the locating tag is depressed using a small screwdriver blade.

and channels for the locking tags. The channels have small steps to lock the tags in place (Fig 42).

Once the connector has been attached to the wire it is simply pushed into the plug body until the tag clicks into place (Fig 43).

The connector is now correctly aligned and cannot push back out of the plug body (Fig 44). If you ever need to remove it a fine screwdriver can be used to fold back the locking tag so that the connector can be carefully pulled out of the plug.

I used multiplugs to isolate the individual circuits from my fuse and relay box (Fig 45). This also enabled me to wire and mount the whole assembly first then connect it into the harness when complete.

My modular fuse and relay box showing the multiplugs used to quickly connect up the individual circuits.

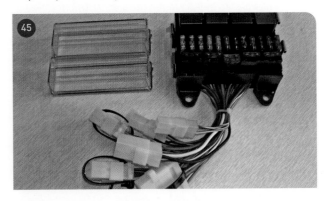

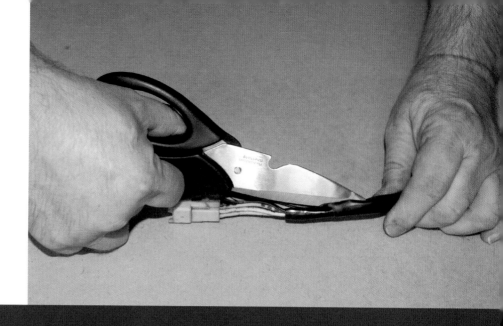

12 Modifying An Existing Loom

Altering and re-sheathing a wiring loom

By now you will have read through the preceding chapters and decided what components you are going to use in your car, where they will be placed and how they will be positioned. If you are simply re-fitting the original loom or a factory replacement back into the unaltered car then no modifications should be necessary. But if you have upgraded, modified, simplified or augmented the electrical system in some way then clearly the original loom will no longer be suitable. If the electrical system changes are minor and your original loom is still in good condition, you will probably be able to modify it to suit. This chapter explains how this is done.

If you have removed components, such as interior lights and door switches for example, then you could simply leave the redundant wires and connectors in the loom and insulate, then tape up, the loose ends. This is not a particularly satisfactory solution though and not one which I

would recommend. The neater and more professional option is to remove unwanted wires from the loom altogether.

Similarly if you wish to add components, such as an audio system, an electric radiator fan or a 2-speed wiper system then you could just tape or cable tie the additional wires to the outside of the existing loom. This would leave them exposed to abrasion or snagging though, so once again this would not be my first choice. The better option by far, if you need to modify a wiring harness, is to remove the outer sheath from the loom, remove or add the required wires and re-wrap the loom when the modifications are complete.

The first step is to remove the outer covering from the section of the harness you intend to modify (Fig 1-4). Early wiring looms were wrapped with a cloth tape which was slightly sticky due to the bitumen based coating applied to make it water resistant. When this is unwound it leaves a

This is a sub section of a main wiring loom. This section leads to a steering column switch.

The loom is protected by PVC sleeving but has been modified with adhesive PVC tape at the open end.

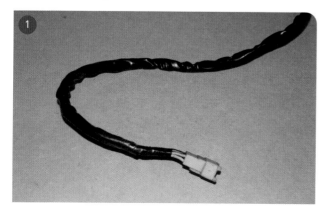

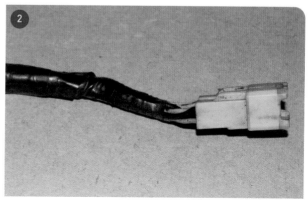

sticky black deposit on the wires. Fortunately this can be cleaned off with white spirit or WD40. This type of harness tape is still available but thankfully was later replaced by non adhesive PVC tape which is much easier to remove and can also be reused if necessary.

If you wish to renew the harness tape always use the non-adhesive type. This allows some flexibility in the harness so that it can be formed into place. Adhesive PVC tape will make the harness difficult to fit and eventually the adhesive will start to creep and make the harness messy in use. If the harness is protected by PVC sleeving or semi-rigid trunking, this will have to be cut or split to remove it (Fig 4). It can be renewed or replaced when the modifications are complete.

Once the outer sleeving has been removed, the individual wires will be visible. Before you go any further, check all the wires for damage to the insulation through abrasion or for cracking due to age. You may need to clean them with white spirit to inspect them thoroughly. Also check the connectors for corrosion or breakage. Replace them if necessary. If there is a significant amount of damage it may be worth considering a new loom. If the loom is serviceable you can

continue with the modifications. The wires will probably still be held together by single wraps of tape at intervals along the harness (Fig 5). These are used to retain the wires in the loom during initial assembly until the outer covering is fitted.

If you cut all of these ties the loom will fall apart, so a better option is to cut them one at a time, add or remove the wires involved in your modifications then re-tape that section of the harness before you move on (Fig 6-7). This will retain the integrity and shape of the harness after your modifications. You can use adhesive PVC tape or self-amalgamating tape here. It will be covered by the outer sheath when the loom is finished. It may be better to fit the connectors or plugs to your additional wires after you have fitted the outer covering. Your choice of sheathing is more limited if the connectors are already attached.

When you have completed all your alterations, the outer covering of the harness needs to be replaced or renewed. Personally I would always use new harness tape, trunking, sleeving or wrap (Fig 8-11). It will be easier to fit as it will be more flexible than used material and it will offer better long-term protection. You do not need to use the original type of

The non-standard PVC tape is being unwrapped here. This would also have to be done to expose tape wrapped wiring looms too.

The wraps of tape hold the wires in place during the assembly of the loom. Cut them one at a time to insert or remove wires.

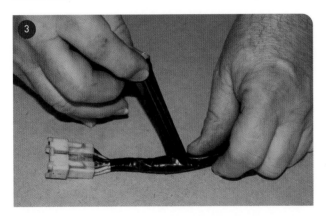

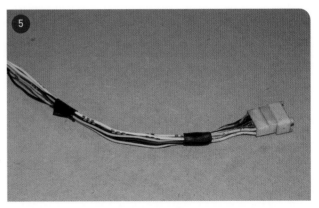

The PVC sleeving needs to be removed too. To do this it needs to be split along its length. New sheathing will be needed when the modifications are complete.

With the tape wrap removed, the new wire (red/black) can be inserted. Fortunately there was a spare socket in the multiplug which could be used.

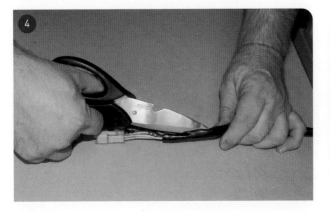

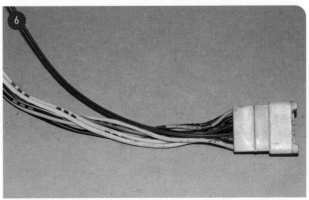

sheathing when you re-cover the loom. There is quite a choice of sleeving materials now (Fig 12).

Convoluted Trunking – This is semi-rigid nylon tubing with stiffening ridges running around the outer circumference. It can be solid or split along its length. The solid variety is less

The tape wraps are replaced as the new wire is fitted into the loom.

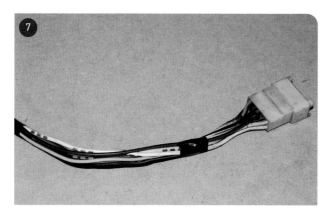

Non-adhesive PVC loom tape is being used to wrap the harness. The tape is stretched slightly and the wraps are overlapped by around 6mm to 8mm.

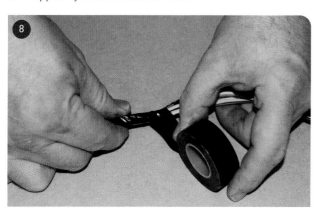

This is the completed loom. The final wrap of tape is secured with adhesive tape or self amalgamating tape.

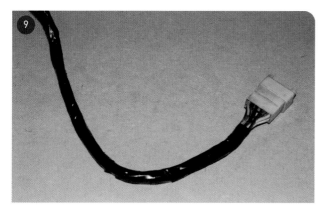

useful for pre-assembled looms as the wires have to be fed in from one end (Fig 13). This may not be possible with a finished loom which has its plugs and connectors already attached.

The split variety is very easy to use (Fig 14). It is simply cut

As an alternative, Twistwrap sleeving could be used. The tube is opened up along the split and fitted around the loom. It springs closed again after fitting.

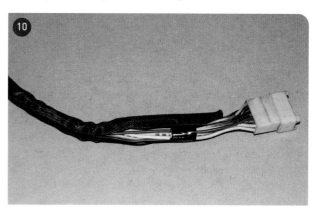

Tape or cable ties can be used to secure the sleeving once it is fitted. Self amalgamating tape has been used here to seal the end of the sleeving.

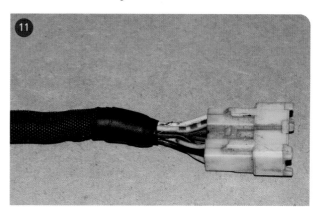

Harness sheathing materials. Convoluted trunking, PVC sleeving, spiral binding, braided sleeving, heat shrink tubing, harness tape and self amalgamating tape.

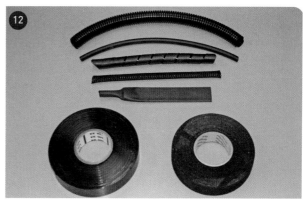

to length and wrapped around the wiring harness. It is sprung so that it will close up around the wires if the correct size is chosen. It can be retained by cable ties.

Available sizes range from 6mm to 24mm bore. End fittings and 'T' pieces are also obtainable.

PVC sleeving – This is basically smooth walled PVC tubing (Fig 15). The wiring needs to be fed in from one end, so once again it is less suitable for finished looms with connectors already attached.

It works well on bare looms and may also be used to protect sub-sections you have added to a loom if you fit it before you attach the connectors. It is available in bore sizes between 5mm and 25mm.

Spiral binding – This is a semi-rigid PVC spiral which is wrapped around the bundle of wires (Fig 16). It does not fully cover the wires unless wrapped very tightly so it does not offer complete protection from dirt and abrasion, but it can be easily applied to pre-assembled looms too. It expands as it is fitted, so only two sizes are needed. The 6mm bore size will fit wire bundles from 5mm to 25mm diameter and the 12mm bore size will cover looms from 10mm to 50mm diameter.

As it is fitted to larger looms the spiral expands in diameter but shortens in length, so allow for this when you cut the material. Longer lengths are also time consuming to fit as the whole length of the material has to be wound along the loom one turn at a time.

Braided sleeving – This is a woven polyester sleeving which can be expanded slightly, like Chinese handcuffs, to aid fitting (Fig 17). It has the same limitations as the other sleeving systems, in that it is not suitable for looms which are already assembled with connectors attached, but can be easily fitted to bare looms. The polyester material has good abrasion resistance but the woven construction is not waterproof.

The cut ends can fray (Fig 18) but this can be prevented using heat shrink tubing, self amalgamating tape or by melting the cut ends with a cigarette lighter or soldering iron.

Bore sizes range from 6m to 12mm but each size has a slight tolerance of 2mm either way. There is a heat resistant version of this sleeving made in acrylic coated fibreglass (Fig 19/20).

It can withstand temperatures up to 150deg C. The range of sizes is more limited. It is available in 4mm, 6mm and

Solid convoluted trunking. This can only be fitted before connectors have been attached to the wires.

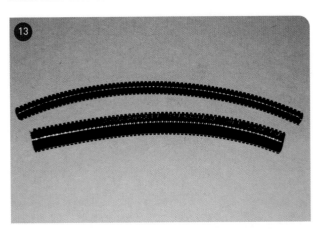

PVC sleeving. There is very little expansion with this sleeving so choose a large enough size or it can be difficult to fit. It is more flexible when warm.

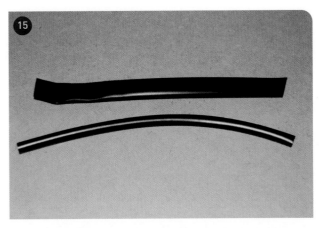

Split convoluted trunking. This can be fitted onto a completed loom and held in place with cable ties. Wires can be led out at any point.

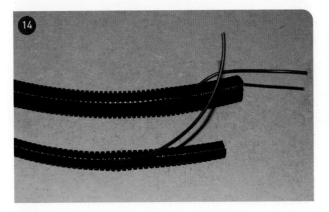

Spiral binding. This can be wound around completed looms to bind and protect them but it does take some time to fit.

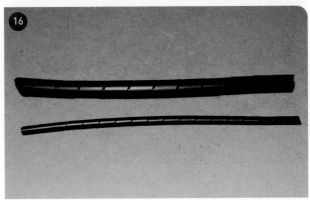

8mm diameters.

Twistwrap sleeving – This is a tightly woven split polyester sleeving (Fig 21).

It can be wrapped round new or pre-assembled harnesses and has enough 'spring' to re-form its shape and close the gap again once fitted (Fig 22).

It is very easy to fit, does not fray and is suitable for

bundles of wire 1.5 times its nominal bore diameter. Cable ties or self-amalgamating tape can be used to permanently secure the sleeving once fitted. It is available in bore sizes from 5mm to 16mm.

Slit harness wrap – This is a polypropylene sleeving which, as its name suggests, is split along its length for easy fitting to new or pre-assembled looms, but which closes up and

Braided sleeving can expand to slide over bundles of wires but really needs to be fitted before plugs and connectors are attached. It looks good when fitted.

The heat resistant fibreglass weave is visible in this photograph.

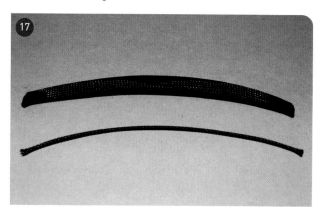

The ends of the woven braid need to be sealed by melting them together with a soldering iron or cigarette lighter.

Twistwrap sleeving is woven split tubing. It is suitable for fitting to completed looms.

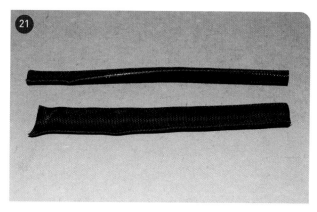

Heat resistant sleeving can withstand higher temperatures than the standard version.

There is enough 'spring' in the tubing for it to close up around bundles of wires once it is fitted. Cable ties will hold it in place.

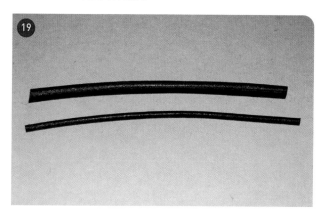

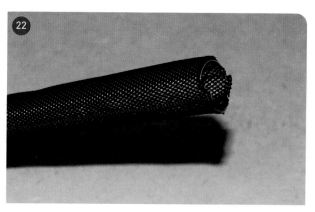

locks around the wire bundle once fitted (Fig 23/24).

A special tool is available, at a very reasonable price, to aid the fitting of the sleeving. It does not completely cover the loom so it does not offer complete protection from dirt and abrasion but allows wires to be led out of the loom easily for connectors, sub harnesses and junctions. It is available in 10mm and 16mm sizes.

Harness tape – This is a thin non adhesive PVC tape available in rolls 19mm (3/4in) or 25mm (1in) wide (Fig 25). It is wound around the harness at a slight angle with each wrap overlapping the previous one by 6-8mm.

The tape can be stretched slightly as it is wrapped to produce some tension and grip. The loose end of the final wrap can be secured by adhesive PVC tape, heat shrink tubing or self-amalgamating tape.

Self-amalgamating tape – This tape resembles the early bitumen version but is made from Polyisobutylene (PIB). The tape is 25mm (1in) wide and has a plastic backing along its entire length (Fig 26).

When the backing is removed the tape is soft and flexible.

It is stretched gently to activate it then wrapped around the wire or the harness. The tape will amalgamate to form a one piece watertight seal. It is particularly useful for sealing cable joints where heat shrink tubing cannot be slid into place.

Heat shrink sleeving – This is a semi-rigid polyolefin sleeving which, when heated with a hot air gun or carefully with a cigarette lighter flame, will shrink to about half its original diameter (Fig 27). It is available in various colours and a range of diameters from 3mm to 25mm.

An adhesive lined version is also available. This type shrinks to a third of its original diameter and the adhesive lining melts then re-hardens to produce a watertight joint around cable joints or woven sleeving (Fig 28). I have also used this material to prevent fraying on braided steel hoses (Fig 29).

With the harness modifications completed and the sleeving replaced, the loom can be fitted into the car. You can trim your modified wiring to length and fit the connectors now if you chose not to do so earlier.

The procedure described above is probably the preferred

This slit harness wrap can be fitted to fully assembled looms but the semi-rigid plastic can be difficult to open without the special tool.

Harness tape is the traditional loom sheathing material. It is easy to use and produces a good finish but provides very little abrasion protection.

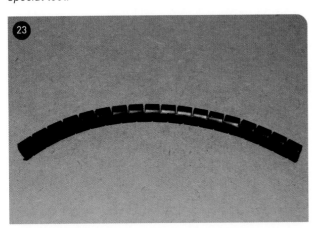

The overlapped tabs click into place making the tubing effectively solid.

Self-amalgamating tape is useful for sealing joints in wires and finishing the ends of loom sheathing.

option if your original loom is in good condition and the modifications you need to make are minor. If there is minor damage or corrosion in the loom it can be repaired while you are making the modifications. If there is significant damage or the modifications you need to make are more extensive, you need to consider whether a complete new loom is a better proposition.

Various sizes and colours of heat shrink sleeving. When heated it will shrink to half its original diameter but the length remains unchanged.

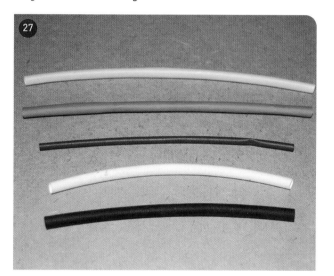

This is self-adhesive heat shrink sleeving. It is lined with a hot-melt adhesive and can produce watertight joints on cables.

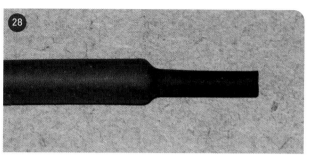

The cut ends of this stainless steel braiding have been sealed to prevent fraying using self adhesive heat shrink sleeving.

13 Choosing A New Loom

Rewiring options

There are many reasons why your original loom may not be useable in your restored, rebuilt or modified car. It may be that it is too old or damaged to be serviceable. Even PVC insulation slowly degrades and hardens with age or exposure to heat. It may be that the degree of modification required to make the loom fit the new car makes it impractical to use the original wiring. You may not even have a donor loom. Modern kit cars tend not to use single donor vehicles anymore. Instead they are often supplied with a package of mechanical parts which may not include a wiring harness. Whatever the reason, if you decide to fit a new wiring harness, there are a number of options open to you.

Having the car professionally wired

If after reading through this book, you still decide that wiring and electrics are not for you then you will have to get someone else to wire your car for you. If you are lucky there may be someone within your particular branch of the motoring fraternity or your owners club that can help you out, but if not you will have to look around for a professional auto electrician in your area who offers this service. Surprisingly, although there are a number of companies willing to build looms or supply parts, not many people offer a full rewiring service.

Wiring a car is time consuming. It would not be unreasonable for an auto-electrician to quote for 40-50 hours labour plus parts if he has to design, manufacture and install a complete vehicle wiring loom from scratch. He would also need access to the vehicle during this time to measure, plan and fit the loom. Clearly this is not going to be a cheap option. The result, however, should be a car wired to at least production car standards. Hopefully the contents of

this book will enable you to make an informed choice about who you select to carry out this work.

Have a look at the components and materials they use. Are they of the quality you would expect? Get a good look at a finished loom. Are you happy with the final product? If possible, contact previous customers to see if they are satisfied with the work that was done for them. Finally make sure that the auto electrician will provide you with a clear wiring diagram for the completed system when it is finished. You may need this in the future should any work be required on the system.

Fitting a manufacturer's loom

When you are stripping a vehicle down prior to a rebuild it is

This is one of the reference photos I took when I was stripping down my bike. It shows the colours of the wires which connect to the two ignition coils.

vital that you label every plug and wire as you disconnect it. Cheap digital cameras have made it practical to take detailed photographs to supplement these labels (Fig 1).

You should also make notes or take photographs of the way the wiring loom is routed through the car. Save any grommets used to protect wires as they pass through panels. Before you remove the wires from any multi-plugs, make a sketch or take a photograph showing the positions of the wires in the plug body (Fig 2). Make sure the position of any locating tags or keyways are marked too.

If you are fitting a new OEM or replica wiring loom to a restored or rebuilt vehicle then it should be routed in exactly the same way as the original harness, using existing mounting points and access passages through body panels. By comparing the labelling and photographs of the old loom with the equivalent connectors on the new loom, and checking all the connections against the standard wiring diagram, you should be able to reconnect every plug and wire exactly as it was on the original harness. Each time you make a connection it is a good idea to pack the terminals with silicone grease to waterproof them and prevent corrosion. Vaseline is an alternative favoured by some people.

If you are building a kit car and have chosen to use the wiring harness sold by the kit manufacturer then the process is very similar to that described above, except that any notes or photographs taken during the stripdown will not be directly applicable to the new wiring. Hopefully the new loom will be fully labelled and detailed fitting instructions will be

Details of the multi-plugs which carry the wiring to the instruments, switches and front lighting on the bike.

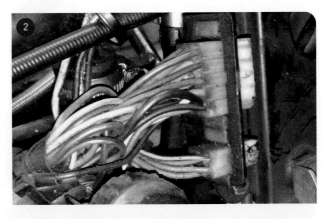

provided by the manufacturer, making this a fairly simple job.

The disadvantage to using the loom provided by the manufacturer is the lack of flexibility and customising options. Unless you have used all the components recommended and possibly sold by the manufacturer and mounted or positioned them as instructed, the loom or its connectors will not match up correctly and will need to be modified to suit. This rather negates the point of using the new loom in the first place.

Some kit car manufacturers, such as Westfield, offer alternative looms for the different engine options available, but in general your choice of components like instruments

This is the basic plan for a front-engined vehicle which Rapidfit supply to customers requiring a bespoke wiring loom.

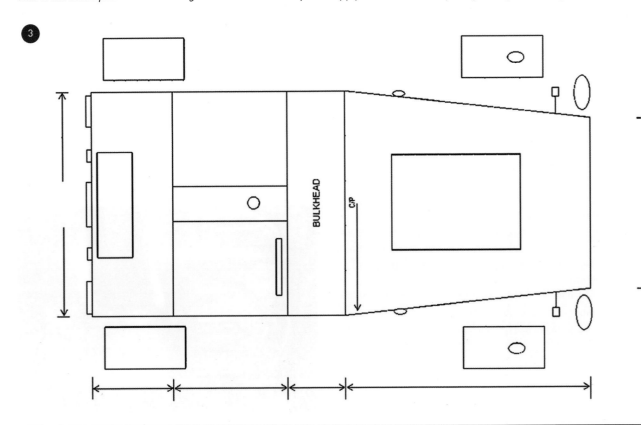

and switches will be restricted. If you are happy with this restriction then this option should be fairly straightforward to fit and will give a professional looking wiring job which should be fully compliant with IVA regulations. Prices will vary with the manufacturer and with the quality of the product but at the time of writing a Westfield loom for a Zetec engine kit is around £260.

Fitting a bespoke loom

Even if your car is customised, a kit car or even a complete one-off, it is still possible to have a bespoke wiring loom made for it. You will have to do more of the initial work with this option but the finished result should be a professional wiring harness made specifically for your car. Ideally all the electrical components should be fitted in the vehicle or at least temporarily located in place so that you can measure all the necessary dimensions and supply them to the loom manufacturer. You will also need to decide where the harness will pass through panels and allow for this in your measurements.

The manufacturer will make the loom exactly to your measurements so make sure you get them right before you send them off to him. The old adage 'measure twice, cut once' springs to mind here. It is worth drawing out a basic plan of your car with all the electrical components and dimensions marked on it as shown in the planning section of

chapter 7. Rapidfit Looms supply these to their customers for both mid and front engined vehicles (Fig 3).

The bespoke loom, when it arrives, should be fully labelled and should have detailed fitting instructions. If you have supplied the manufacturer with details of the connectors required on each wire, they should be already fitted on delivery but if such specifics were not available the loom may require final trimming to length and the required connectors crimping in place. Actually fitting the loom into the car should be straightforward although you will have to decide on the various attachment points throughout the car.

Fitting a universal loom

This is a half-way stage between having a bespoke loom made for your car and manufacturing your own from scratch. Universal looms, as their name suggests, are designed to fit as wide a range of cars as possible using a small number of basic designs (Fig 4).

In order to achieve this aim, the builder has to do more of the finishing work themselves. The loom manufacturers will try to include wiring for all the normal components found in a vehicle, but if you have fitted anything unusual you may need to add in the odd extra wire. Similarly if your electrical system is stripped down to basics you may wish to remove any redundant circuits before you fit the wiring. To facilitate this, the looms are normally supplied without their final sheathing

This is the Rapidfit modular loom. It is manufactured in four sections with pre-fitted multi-plugs connecting the modules.

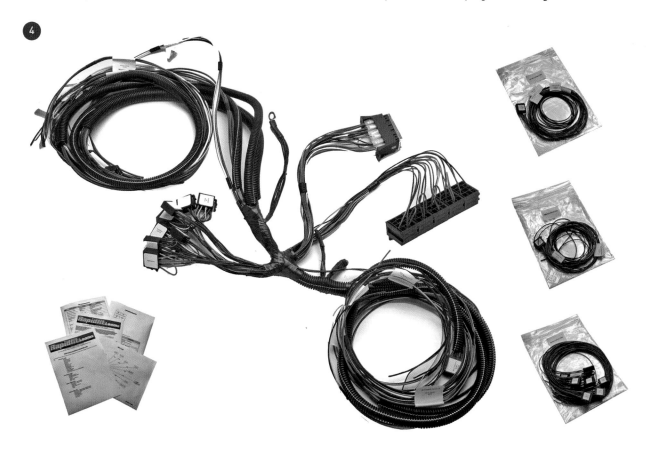

This is a DIN colour coded rear engined Uniloom from Premier Wiring Systems. It is for my VW Beetle based UVA Fugutive.

in place. Wires can be added or removed easily before the loom is completed by fitting the harness tape or trunking.

Similarly the wires leading to the individual components or systems are deliberately left over-long to maximise fitting options. When the routing of the loom is finalised these wires can be trimmed to length and the correct connectors can be crimped in place. All the individual wires and plugs are labelled to show their function and detailed fitting instructions are provided. These looms are very comprehensive and usually include pre-wired fuse boxes and relays (Fig 5-9). A number of kit car manufacturers offer these universal looms as an option with their kits.

Obviously one design cannot possibly fit every car, so universal looms are normally available in at least two versions to cater for front-engined or rear-engined cars. At least one manufacturer offers a choice of wiring colour codes. Its looms are available in Lucas, Ford or DIN wiring colours. The use of modular looms increases their versatility and also simplifies the fitting and routing of the loom. In my opinion universal looms represent excellent value for money. The cost of a universal loom (£120 to £180 at the time of writing) is not a great deal more than the cost of the individual wires and components bought separately.

This is the two piece loom. They also make a four piece alternative. Connectors, grommets and a crimping tool are included.

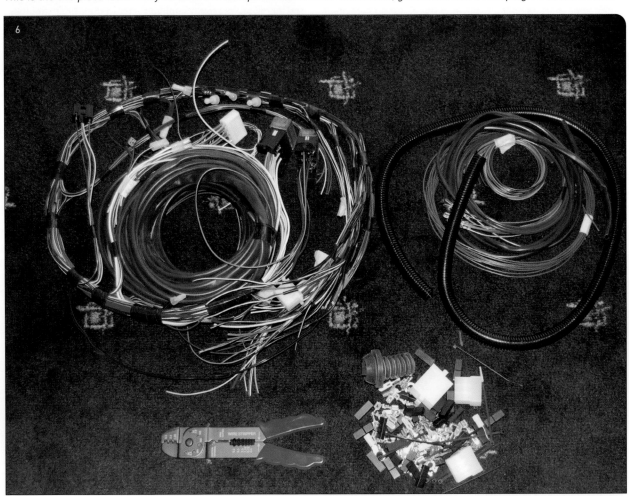

Fitting your own custom made loom

If you have decided not to go for any of the previous options, then the only choice left to you is to design, make and fit your own custom made wiring harness. This is obviously the most labour intensive of the possibilities but is also the least expensive.

Fuse boxes, with fuses, are already attached to the loom.

The wires are labelled to show their destination. These connect to the headlamp relay.

The fitting instructions give full details of the colour coding and destination for each individual wire.

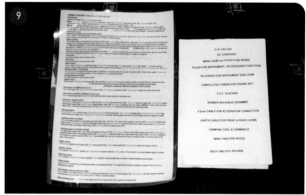

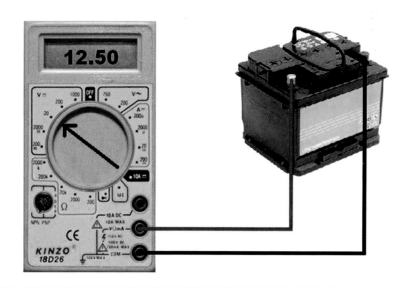

14 Testing Your Wiring

Non-destructive testing

If you are brave or confident, you can simply complete the wiring, connect up the battery and switch on the various circuits whilst checking for correct functions, smoke or flame.

If, like me, you like to double-check everything, then a multimeter is invaluable (Fig 1).

A simple test lamp can be used to check that power is reaching specific points in the circuit, but not until the car battery has been connected. A multimeter can also do this but, since it has its own internal power source, it can also be used at a much earlier stage in the wiring process, even before the battery is fitted. It can be used to check each individual circuit as it is wired. It is also useful for working out how complex switches function. You can determine which terminals are inter-connected when the actuator is moved through its various positions. Should any circuits not function as expected it can be used to test bulbs, fuses, switches, batteries and charging systems too. Some multimeters are designed specifically for automotive use and may also be able to measure temperature, engine rpm and ignition dwell angle.

Choosing a multimeter

The three basic parameters you may need to measure in vehicle wiring and fault finding are resistance, DC voltage, and, less often, DC current. AC readings are of very limited use in motor vehicle work, but most multimeters will have

A typical general purpose digital multimeter. It has all the functions needed for automotive use plus a few others too. This particular example is supplied with a protective rubber case.

This is a 'digital automotive analyser'. It is a multimeter with some vehicle specific functions such as a tachometer and a dwell meter. Here it is being used to check the battery voltage.

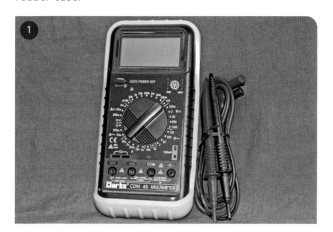

the ability to measure these anyway. Fans, wiper motors and headlamps are high current items so it is important to make sure that the meter is able to measure DC currents of at least 10amps. 20amps is even better but this capacity is not so common in lower priced meters.

A continuity setting is handy but not essential. The continuity function simply means that an internal buzzer will sound when the resistance measured is below a certain value, usually about 50Ω. In practice this means that the buzzer will sound if the probes are connected to either end of an unbroken circuit, wire or fuse. The buzzer is useful as it means that there is no need to keep looking at the display while you are performing this check.

Some meters have a data hold function which 'freezes' the meter reading until it is released. This may be useful in some circumstances but is certainly not essential.

Multimeters are available in either digital or analogue forms. There are advantages and disadvantages to both. Analogue meters react instantly to changes in readings whereas digital ones are more sluggish. Digital meters are easier to use, more accurate and generally are more versatile. They tend to have more functions too.

Multimeters are delicate instruments. They can be damaged if dropped or handled roughly. Many now come with a rubber or flexible plastic outer case or 'holster' which clips round them offering some protection whilst in use. A storage case can be useful too, since the meter will probably only be used occasionally once the wiring is completed.

Using a multimeter

The number of functions available on a multimeter can make them seem complicated to a beginner but in fact, when working with auto electrical systems we rarely use more than two or three of these functions. This is how they are used.

Testing for continuity

This function checks for breaks in a circuit, a blown fuse or a faulty light bulb.

Testing a fuse to see if it has blown. The low resistance reading shows that this fuse is good.

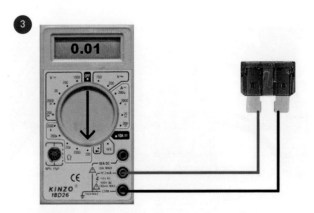

Set the selector switch to the continuity position or, if your meter doesn't have this function, to a low resistance setting (around 200Ω). Check the meter by touching the probes together. The buzzer should sound (continuity setting) and the reading should drop almost to zero.

Checking a fuse – Connect the probes to the two contacts on the fuse (Fig 3). It doesn't matter which way round you connect them. If the fuse is OK the buzzer should sound and the reading will fall to a very low value.

Checking a bulb – Connect the probes to the two contacts on the bulb (Fig 4). It doesn't matter which way round you connect them. If the bulb is OK the buzzer should sound (continuity setting) and the reading will fall. The actual reading will depend on the bulb itself but any low value is fine.

Switch function – Multi function switches such as those for ignition, wipers, or indicators can be tested to find out which terminals are connected as the switch actuator is moved through its different positions. In each switch position,

Testing a bulb to see if it has blown. The actual meter reading will not be zero since the bulb filament does have a low, but measurable resistance. Any low value indicates a working bulb.

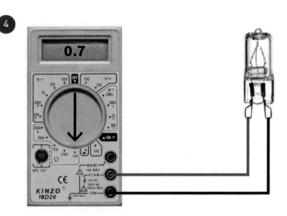

With the switch in each of its positions check the terminals to see which combinations are connected.

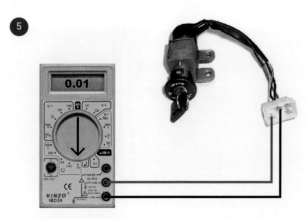

touch the meter probes to pairs of terminals in turn (Fig 5). It doesn't matter which way round you connect them. If the terminals are connected in that switch position the buzzer will sound (continuity setting) and the reading will fall to a very low value. If the switch is quite complex it may be wise to make a note of your results. An ignition switch, for example, would give results similar to this

Position 0 (off)	No connections
Position 1 (accessories)	Terminals 1 & 2
Position 2 (run)	Terminals 1, 2 & 3
Position 3 (start)	Terminals 1, 3 & 4

Testing for a live supply

This function uses the multimeter like a test lamp but actually measures the voltage present at any point in a circuit. Set the selector switch to measure 20v DC.

Voltage present – Connect the probe on the black wire to a good earthing point. Switch on the circuit being tested. Connect the red probe to the point of the circuit being tested (Fig 6). If the correct live supply is reaching that point in the circuit then the meter should read around 12v. Sometimes ignition coils are fitted with ballast resistors, in which case the reading would only be around 8-10v.

Battery and alternator test – Connect the black lead to the negative battery terminal and the red lead to the positive. The reading should be around 12.5v. To test the charging system start the engine. The reading should rise to about 14.5v if the charging circuit is working correctly.

Measuring current

To measure the current flowing in a circuit the meter must be connected in series in the circuit. Part of the circuit needs to be disconnected so that the meter can be connected across the resulting gap.

Set the selector switch to the 10A DC position on your meter. Connect the red probe wire to the 10A socket on your meter. Disconnect one wire in the circuit you want to test.

Connect the probe wires to the two exposed ends of the resulting gap in the circuit. Make sure the red probe wire is connected to the positive side of the circuit and the black probe to the negative side (Fig 8). Switch on the circuit and quickly check the meter to see the current flowing in the circuit. If the reading is over 10A switch it off again even more quickly! On most multimeters the 10A circuit is not fused so if too much current flows the meter will be damaged, but most have an overload facility which allows a few seconds grace before damage occurs.

Testing a newly completed circuit

Where possible I try to test each circuit as soon as it is installed. The multimeter, with its own power supply, makes this possible even before the battery is fitted. You can even test each wire separately if you wish but it will make your overall progress slower.

To illustrate the process I will use the sample heater circuit outlined in chapter 8 (Fig 09).

Testing the battery voltage. With the engine running a healthy charging system should raise the reading to around 14.5 volts.

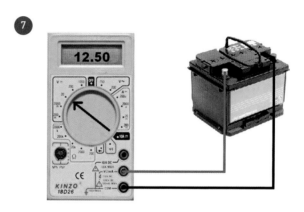

To measure the current flowing in a circuit the meter must be connected in series with the components in the circuit. To do this you will have to break into the circuit somewhere. You must also make sure the polarity is correct.

Testing the power supply to the ignition coil. Make sure you have a good earth connection for the meter.

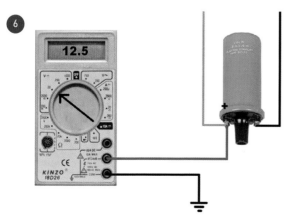

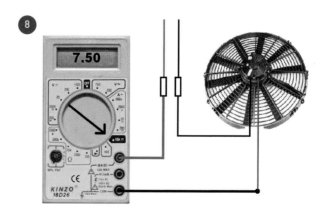

1. Use the continuity setting if your meter has this function or set your multimeter to a low resistance scale. Around 200Ω should be fine. Connect the positive (red) lead of your multimeter to point 1, the point where the ignition switch feed connects to the battery. This lead will remain attached to this point throughout the test. The negative (black) lead is then used to test the rest of the circuit by connecting it to each of the other points in the following sequence.

2. Connect to point 2. There should be almost zero resistance here (continuity).

3. Connect to point 3. With the ignition off there should be an infinite resistance (open circuit). With the ignition in the 'run' position there should be almost zero resistance. Leave the ignition switch on for the rest of the test.

4. Connect to point 4. There should be almost zero resistance here.

5. Connect to point 5. There should be almost zero resistance here. Check the fuse and its connections if this is not correct.

6. Connect to point 6. There should be almost zero resistance here.

7. Connect to point 7. With the heater switch off there should be an infinite resistance (open circuit). With the switch in the 'slow' position there should be almost zero resistance unless a resistor is used to slow the fan down, in which case there may be a low but measurable resistance here.

8. Connect to point 8. With the heater switch off there should be an infinite resistance (open circuit). With the switch in the 'fast' position there should be almost zero resistance.

9. Connect to point 9. With the heater switch off there should be an infinite resistance (open circuit). With the switch in the 'slow' position the resistance should be much the same as it was in test 7 in this sequence.

10. Connect to point 10. With the heater switch off there should be an infinite resistance (open circuit). With the switch in the 'fast' position there should be almost zero resistance. Leave the heater switch on 'fast' for the last part of the test.

11. Connect to point 11. The resistance will not be zero as the current is now passing through the fan motor but as long as it is a measurable value and not infinite (open circuit) then the wiring is fine.

By testing the circuit in the above sequence it is possible not only to identify faults but also to isolate the fault to a small part of the circuit. If, at any stage, the reading on the multimeter is not correct, check out that section of the circuit for bad connections or broken wires. Loose or faulty fuses or bulbs will show up in these tests too.

Testing each circuit on completion will mean that hopefully, when you do complete the whole of the wiring and finally connect the battery, all the electrical systems will work perfectly. As a final safeguard though it is worth temporarily fitting a fuse of around 30A in the main power feed to the ignition and light switches. A maxifuse will do the job nicely. This will allow you to connect up the battery and test most of the main systems in the knowledge that, if you have made a serious mistake anywhere, the temporary fuse will blow before any wiring is damaged. Unfortunately you cannot use a fuse like this in the starter system as the currents carried are too high.

The testing points and sequence on a typical heater circuit.

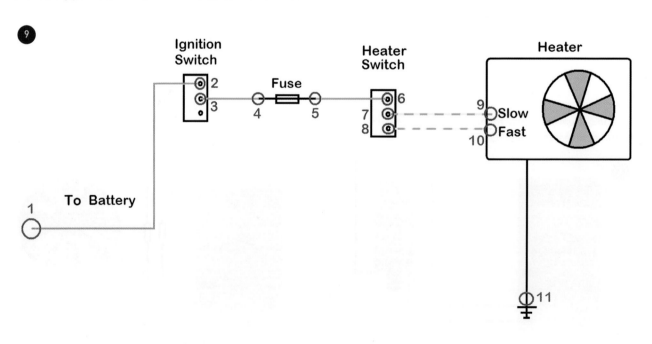

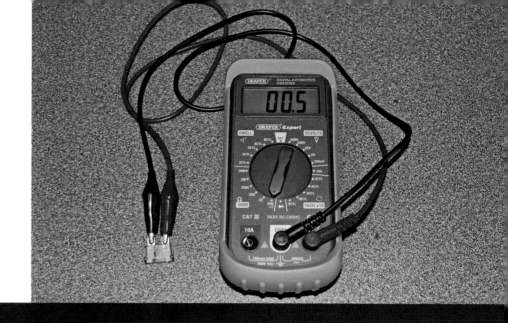

15 Fault Finding
Testing methods

As mentioned earlier in this book it is a fact that, apart from flat tyres and running out of fuel, the most common causes of vehicle breakdowns are electrical in nature.

If you have followed the advice given in this book when you designed, assembled and tested your wiring then all should be well and your electrical systems should give you many years of trouble-free service. Electricity is tricky stuff though. I have no real faith in any system that can be mended simply by jiggling things a bit. For this reason I felt it necessary to include a chapter on tracing and fixing electrical faults in the hope that it will never be needed.

Mechanical problems can usually be spotted easily and any damage can be repaired or replaced. Electricity is

A simple 12v test light. The bulb is in the handle. The sharp probe can be pushed through the insulation of a wire to contact the copper conductor.

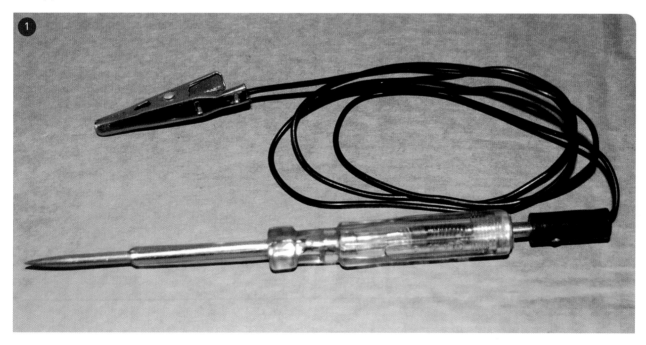

invisible so it needs a whole different approach to troubleshooting. A systematic approach is needed along with a couple of specialised tools.

Test Light

A test light is simply a 12v bulb mounted with two connecting leads or a connecting lead and a probe. It is a very cheap tool but is also easy to make if you have a spare bulb and holder lying around in your garage. It is used to check that power is reaching various points in a circuit when the circuit is switched on. It is a good idea to check the test light before use, just in case the bulb has blown. It would be very frustrating to spend time trying to diagnose an electrical fault with a broken test light. Connect the light across the two battery terminals and check that the bulb lights up before you start your testing.

Jumper leads

Jumper leads, in this application, are not the big heavy leads used to connect car batteries together in an emergency. They

Jumper leads can be made from any spare lengths of wire you happen to have saved. They need to be around 2-3m long and a few could be made with various connectors on the end to increase their usefulness.

A typical multimeter in use. It is being used to check a fuse for continuity. It is set to measure resistance and the low reading shows the fuse is intact.

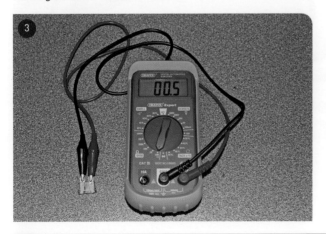

are normal car wiring leads 2-3m long with suitable connectors on the ends to enable them to by-pass sections of a faulty circuit and carry a direct live feed to a component to see if it is working correctly. They can also be used to directly earth a component if a faulty earth connection is suspected. The jumper lead needs to be thick enough to carry whatever current the component being tested normally uses. As an extra safety feature you could wire an in-line fuse into your jumper lead.

Multimeter

In my opinion a multimeter is an essential diagnostic tool for electrical work. It can do the same job as a test lamp but will also show the actual voltage present at any point in a circuit. It can check the continuity of a circuit, bulb or fuse without the need for an external power supply and, if required, can measure how much current is flowing in a circuit. With prices starting at around £6 for an analogue meter and £10 for a digital version, a multimeter should definitely be part of your toolkit.

A common sense approach

If an electrical fault occurs you can save yourself a lot of time by applying basic reasoning or common sense. If, for example, one brake light has failed but the other one is still working as normal, then the fault is unlikely to be in the battery, fuse or switch. It is more likely to be in the bulb, the bulb holder, the wire carrying the power or the earth to that individual bulb. If, on the other hand, the indicators have stopped working completely on both sides of the car, it is very unlikely that all four bulbs will have blown together. The fault is more likely to be in one of the components that they all share such as the fuse, the switch or the flasher unit.

When you are testing a circuit, try all the possible combinations of the circuit and note down the results. The more information you can get the easier it is to diagnose the fault. Check that only one circuit is affected. If two or more circuits fail, do they share a common fuse or power supply? It is not unknown for faults in one circuit to affect others. The classic example is that of a poor earth on a rear indicator light which causes the corresponding brake light to flash instead, as the circuit earths itself through the brake light filament. The wiring diagram for the vehicle is helpful here too. This is why you need to make sure that one is supplied with whatever loom that you buy or why you must draw your own diagram if you make your own loom. It is impossible to give specific procedures for every possible electrical fault so instead I will try to outline general fault finding strategies.

Failure of a single component

In the event of only one component in a circuit being affected, start at that component and work backwards, one step at a time, to the fuse, switch and power supply.

• Is the actual component itself faulty? Bulbs can be checked with a multimeter. Other components can be tested by using a jumper lead to supply power to them directly. If it still does not work it is likely to be the component itself which is faulty.

- Is power reaching the component? Earth one lead of a test light or a multimeter set on the 20v DC scale. Use the probe or second lead to see whether a 12v supply is reaching the component when all the switches are on. If not check the wiring as described below.
- Is the component earthed? Use a jumper lead to connect the body of the component or its earth terminal to a good earthing point on the car and check its operation again.
- Is the wiring faulty? Earth one lead of a test light or a multimeter set on the 20v DC scale. Working backwards from the component to the power supply use the probe or second lead to check each point in the circuit to see whether a 12v supply is reaching that point when all the switches are on. This will enable you to identify which section of the wiring has the fault.

Failure of all the components in a circuit

If all the components in a circuit stop working the most likely cause is a fault in the power supply. Check the fuse first.

- Is power reaching the switch? Using a test light or multimeter check that a 12v supply is reaching the main switch of the faulty circuit.
- Is power reaching the fuse? Check, using the test light or multimeter, that a 12v supply is leaving the switch and reaching the input side of the fuse. If not the switch may be faulty.
- Is the fuse intact? Check visually, or using a multimeter set to read resistance, that the fuse is sound. Check the fuse holders for dirt or corrosion.
- Is power leaving the fuse? Check, using the test light or multimeter, that a 12v supply is available at the output side of the fuse. If not the fuse housing may be faulty.
- Is power passing through any other common components? Using the test light or multimeter, in conjunction with the wiring diagram, check any other components in the circuit such as flasher units or voltage stabilisers to see that power is entering and leaving them.

Intermittent faults

These are the hardest faults to trace even for professionals. You can guarantee that when you take your car to a garage with an intermittent electrical fault, the fault will be absent all day and will not appear until the moment you start to drive home. I once owned a FWD Ford Escort which always developed a bad misfire after around 100 miles at 70mph. Needless to say, the fault could never be duplicated for diagnosis.

Once again, common sense is your best hope. First do all the obvious checks.

- Check for loose, dirty or corroded connections.
- Check for loose or corroded fuses and their holders.
- Check for fraying or chafing of the harness outer cover or the wire insulation.
- Try wiggling the harness wherever it is accessible to see if this duplicates the fault.

Take careful note of the conditions under which the fault appears.

- Is it brought on by engine heat? Is it worse in hot weather?
- Is it affected by rain or wet roads?
- Does it occur when cornering or going over bumps?
- Does throttle position make a difference. Is it worse with the engine under heavy load?

If you can duplicate the fault or isolate the conditions under which it occurs then you are well on the way to diagnosing it.

Repeated failure of a fuse

Occasionally fuses blow for no apparent reason. The fuse can be replaced and the circuit functions normally again. If the same fuse blows regularly then there is a definite fault. If could be that the original fuse was of the wrong value, but you must never fit a fuse with a higher value than specified just to stop it blowing. If the fuse is in a lighting circuit, check that the bulbs fitted are of the correct wattage. Replacing two 60w headlight bulbs with two 100w bulbs will raise the current demand from 10 amps to almost 17 amps. A 15 amp fuse would be fine for the original fitment but would not be able to cope with the uprated bulbs.

If replacement fuses blow as soon as the circuit is switched on the most likely cause is a short circuit. Somewhere in the wiring a 12v supply wire is touching a direct earth. The most likely cause is a loose, chaffed or burnt wire. Remove the fuse and connect a test lamp across the two fuse terminals. Switch on the circuit. The test lamp bulb should light. Starting at the point in the circuit furthest from the power supply disconnect each component or wire in turn until the test lamp goes out. The short circuit should be somewhere in the last section you disconnected.

A schematic diagram of a typical relay showing the pin layout and the internal connections.

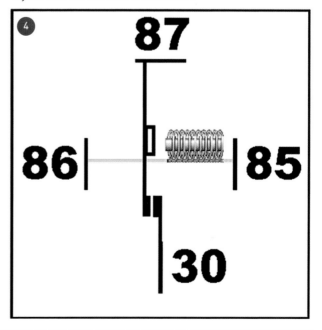

Simply replacing a fuse with one of greater value is unlikely to cure an underlying problem.

Relays

Relays are generally very reliable but, as with all electrical and mechanical components, they do have a finite working life.

The best way to test a relay is to remove it from the car. This is easily done if the relay is fitted into a socket. If the wires are connected directly to the relay make a note of the wire colours and connections so that they can be refitted in the same positions. The wires connected to terminals 30 and 87 are the power leads and will normally be of a heavier gauge than the control wires connected to terminals 85 and 86. You will need a multimeter set to read around 200Ω resistance and two jumper leads.

- Connect the multimeter to terminals 85 and 86. The reading should be low but measurable. Around 100Ω or so is fine. If the resistance is zero or infinite (open circuit) the relay coil is damaged.
- Connect the multimeter to terminals 30 and 87. The internal contacts should be open so the resistance should be infinite (open circuit).
- Take your jumper leads. Connect terminal 85 to a good earth. Connect terminal 86 to a 12v power supply. The battery can be used with care. The relay should 'click' when this connection is made.
- With the jumper leads still connected to the relay connect your multimeter to terminals 30 and 87 again. This time the internal contacts should be closed so the reading should be close to zero. A higher resistance here may mean that the internal contact surfaces are pitted.

Common faults in specific circuits

Batteries – Most modern batteries are maintenance free and do not require topping up with distilled water. All you need to do is to keep the terminals and connections clean, free from corrosion and lightly greased with Vaseline or silicone grease. They are correctly called starting batteries and are not meant to be deeply discharged. Try not to flatten them through overuse. This can damage them very quickly.

Overcharging will also kill a battery, especially the sealed variety. In my experience modern batteries seem to fail quite

suddenly with very little warning. Older batteries would gradually lose their capacity but could be coaxed along for a couple of weeks by recharging every few days. Modern batteries seem to be absolutely fine one day and dead as a doornail the next. They do, however, seem to last much longer overall, so the trade off is definitely in our favour. The working life of a good quality battery is typically three to five years. If you have a problem with a new or recent battery repeatedly going flat over the course of a few days, you may have a fault known as a power drain. Some electrical items such as clocks, radios and alarms need a constant power supply but only draw a few milliamps so it is unlikely that they would be the cause of the problem. A power drain fault is normally caused by a short circuit or an electrical component not switching off correctly. You can check for a power drain using a multimeter set initially to the 10 amp DC scale.

- Disconnect the earth lead to the battery.
- Connect the black lead of your meter to the negative battery terminal and the red lead to the disconnected end of the original earth lead.
- If there is a current drain it will show up as a reading on the meter.
- One circuit at a time switch off or disconnect any circuits which you know are operating. This includes things like interior lights, clocks, alarms, radio/tape/CD players etc. Check the meter to see if the current drain stops at any point. If it does you have identified the source of the drain.
- If the current drain is still there remove the fuses one at a time checking to see if the current drain stops at any point. If it does, note which circuit was causing the drain. Check out that circuit.
- If the drain is still there after switching off all the ancillary circuits and removing all the fuses then you have no choice but to start disconnecting individual components, one at a time, until you identify the source of the current drain.

Charging system – Alternators are not really user serviceable as far as most of us are concerned and are normally exchanged for a new or reconditioned unit if a fault develops. We can, however, do some simple checks to see if they are functioning correctly.

- Check the alternator connections for tightness, dirt and corrosion and clean if necessary.
- With the engine off use a multimeter to measure the voltage across the battery terminals. Set the meter to the 20v scale and connect the red wire to the positive terminal and the black wire to the negative. The reading should be around 12.5v.
- Start the engine and run it at around 2000 rpm. The reading on the meter should increase to around 14.5v.
- With the engine still running get someone to switch on the headlights. The voltage should drop momentarily then come back up to around 14.5v.

If the voltage, with the engine running, is less than 13v or more than 15v then it is likely that there is a problem with the regulator circuit. Early alternators had an external regulator which could be changed separately but most modern alternators have an internal regulator so if a fault is suspected the whole unit must be renewed.

Starter motors – Modern pre-engaged starter motors normally have very long service lives. Starter problems can normally be traced to a low battery or, more commonly, loose or corroded connections on the heavy duty cables carrying the high starter motor current. If the starter is not operating or only turning very slowly check all the heavy duty cables. Disconnect them at each end. Clean the terminals and the cable ends with a wire brush or something similar then apply a little Vaseline or silicone grease to the terminals and re-assemble them. Tighten them securely. As a guide these are the high current cables normally fitted to a car.

- The earth lead from the battery to the car chassis.
- The power lead from the battery to the solenoid.
- The power lead from the solenoid to the starter (if accessible).
- The earth lead from the engine unit to the chassis.

While you have the Vaseline in your hand it may also be worth cleaning and greasing the terminals connecting the smaller wires to the solenoid too.

Lighting circuits – The most common fault with lighting circuits is simply blown bulbs. Faulty or corroded bulb holders and bad earth connections also cause their fair share of problems. These faults are normally associated with poor location of the lights or connectors allowing water to enter and damage the units. Headlight and dip switches can suffer from erosion of their contact surfaces if relays are not used and even relays themselves can eventually fail due to the same problem.

Indicator circuits – In addition to the common faults associated with all lighting circuits, indicators can also develop faults associated with the flasher unit itself. Indicators flashing at the wrong rate can be due to a faulty flasher unit, the wrong flasher unit, incorrect bulb ratings or the use of LED indicator units without the necessary resistors to simulate the correct load.

Windscreen wipers and washers – It is easy to assume that problems with windscreen wipers are electrical in origin but this may not be the case. Wiper spindles and linkages can run dry and corrode causing them to move sluggishly or even seize solid. Make sure the wiper blades, arms and drive system move freely before moving on to check the electrical circuits. The motor can be damaged if it is switched on with the linkage locked for any reason.

Electrical problems with the wiper system often involve the self-park switch. This switch ensures that no matter where the wipers are on the screen when you switch them off they will always return to their parked position. To achieve this there is a cam operated switch mechanism built into the wiper motor. It is supplied with a live feed and keeps the motor running independently of the main switch until the cam opens the contacts. These switches carry the full motor current and are often quite flimsy in construction. The contacts can erode due to arcing and when the switch stops

Horns are often in exposed areas. Watch for corroded connections here.

working the wipers will no longer self–park. Even more entertaining is the effect produced if the contacts fuse together. This causes the wipers to run constantly as long as the ignition is on.

Windscreen washer pumps are generally reliable and have a low current draw so switches tend to last too. The most common problem with windscreen washers is a physical blockage of the washer jets or pipes caused by sediment or ice.

Cooling fans – Electric radiator fans draw a very high current. Connections need to be clean and free from corrosion. Their position behind the radiator makes this difficult to achieve in the long term so the first place to check in the event of a failure are the connections to the fan motor. Thermostatic switches can also fail, although the use of a relay to carry the fan current will extend the life of their electrical contacts. If you suspect that the thermostatic switch has failed by-pass it with a jumper lead. If the fan operates correctly with the by-pass it is time to fit a new switch.

Horns – Horns tend to be positioned in exposed areas of a vehicle and are subject to adverse weather conditions. Corroded connections and bad earths tend to be the most common problems with car horns. Their internal contacts can also erode over time. There may be an adjustment to deal with this but I have never had any long term success using this facility.

As I said earlier I have included this chapter for completeness but I hope that you will never need to use it.

It is just not possible to list all the faults which can occur in the electrical system of a motor vehicle and therefore equally impossible to give specific instructions on how to trace and correct each one. What I have tried to do in this chapter is to outline the systematic approach needed when chasing down electrical faults. If you approach the process logically, make notes if necessary and think about each step carefully then troubleshooting electrical problems can be as straightforward as any other aspect of a motor vehicle.

Appendix 1
IVA considerations

This appendix covers the areas of the IVA regulations which apply to electrical systems. I do not intend to reproduce the actual IVA regulations here as these are subject to regular revisions which would quickly make this chapter out of date. Instead I will highlight those areas of a vehicle's electrical system which are subject to IVA regulations so that you can check the relevant sections of the rules which are current when you are wiring your car.

03A Fuel tanks. All metal fuel tanks must have an earthing strap to prevent the build up of static electricity.

06 Doors. Rear or top hinged doors need additional security devices and audible warnings to prevent them being left open when driving.

07 Audible warning. All vehicles must have a securely fitted horn which emits a continuous sound. The performance is regulated too.

09D Hydraulic system. A fluid level warning light with a test button is required. You may also need a line pressure warning light. If ABS is fitted this needs a system function warning light too.

10 Electromagnetic compatibility. The HT ignition system must be fitted with approved radio interference suppression equipment.

12 Interior fittings. All switches, control knobs etc within the 'specified zone' must comply with regulations on type and impact resistance.

13A/B Anti-theft/Immobiliser. A vehicle must be fitted with either a mechanical anti-theft device or a built-in electronic immobiliser.

16 Exterior projections. Aerial shafts must be blunted and fitted with a 'fixed end capping'.

17 Speedometer. The vehicle must be fitted with an acceptable type of speedometer. Visibility and accuracy are regulated too.

20 Installation of lights. There are regulations relating to mandatory fitments, switching, colours, positions, visibility and brightness of all lights.

21 Reflectors. Type and position are regulated.

22 Sidelights. Type and position are regulated.

23 Indicators. Regulations govern position, brightness, flash rate, visibility and tell tales.

24 Number plate lamps. Type and position are regulated.

25 Headlamps. Type and position are regulated along with E marks and dip pattern.

26 Front fog lights. Type and position are regulated.

28 Rear fog lights. Type and position are regulated.

29 Reversing lights. Type and position are regulated.

30 Parking lamps. Type and position are regulated.

33 Identification of controls. Specific legends are required for each control. Tell tales are needed for brake warning lights, main beam warning lights and indicator warning lights.

34 Windscreen de-misting. If you have a windscreen,you must have a fan assisted hot air system or an electrically heated screen.

35 Washers/wipers. Regulations specify the swept area, require two speeds with set wipe frequencies and require a self-park capability. The wash bottle capacity is specified and the washer pump must operate for a minimum time even with the jets blocked.

36 Heater. This is optional but if fitted it is subject to some safety regulations concerning hot parts. The air inlet must not draw in exhaust fumes.

General construction. Electrical components must not be subject to either a corrosive environment or be exposed to heat sources likely to cause premature failure. All electrical cables/wires must be free from chaffing and secured at specified intervals unless contained in a secure hollow component. All electrical components must be secure and be of adequate capacity and insulated as required as to prevent short circuiting during operation.

Useful contacts

To download an IVA inspection manual
http://tinyurl.com/65usew

IVA testing stations
http://tinyurl.com/2v7rwn

Appendix 2
Contacts

Harnesses
Auto Sparks, 80-88 Derby Road, Sandiacre, Nottingham NG10 5HU. **T:** 0115 949 7211
E: sales@autosparks.co.uk
W: www.autosparks.co.uk

Premier Wiring Systems, 20 Maritime Lane, Leith, Edinburgh, Midlothian EH6 6RZ.
T: 0131 554 0099
E: sales@premierwiring.co.uk
W: www.premierwiring.co.uk

Rapid fit wiring looms, Unit 3, King Street Building, King Street, Enderby, Leicester, Leicestershire LE19 4NT.
T: 0116 2841050
Available through Stafford Vehicle Components Ltd, 53 Kepler, Off Mariner, Lichfield Road Industrial Estate, Tamworth, Staffordshire B79 7XE.
T: 01827 67714
E: info@s-v-c.co.uk
W: www.s-v-c.co.uk/prod_rapidfit.html

Materials and Components
Ardent Distribution Ltd, Suite E, Cardigan Mills, Lennox Road, Leeds LS4 2BL.
T: 0113 2631418
W: www.ardentdl.com

Auto Electric Supplies Limited, 13 Cross Street, Tenbury Wells, Worcestershire WR15 8EF.
T: 01584 819552
E: info@autoelectricsupplies.co.uk
W: www.autoelectricsupplies.co.uk

Car Builder Solutions, Redlands, Lindridge Lane, Staplehurst, Kent TN12 0JJ.
T: 01580 891309
E: sales@carbuildersolutions.co.uk
W: www.cbsonline.co.uk

Europa Specialist Spares, Fauld Industrial Park, Burton-on-Trent, Staffordshire DE13 9HR.
T: 01283 815609
E: info@europaspares.com
W: www.europaspares.com

IEM Services, Unit 1, Agar Way, Pool, Redruth, Cornwall TR15 3SF.
T: 01209 214086
W: www.thewiringproject.co.uk
E: info@iem-services.co.uk

Premier Wiring Systems, Unit 6, Camps Industrial Est., East Calder, West Lothian EH27 8DF.
T: 01506 883886
E: sales@premierwiring.co.uk
W: www.premierwiring.co.uk

Stafford Vehicle Components Ltd, 53 Kepler, Off Mariner, Lichfield Road Industrial Estate, Tamworth, Staffordshire B79 7XE.
T: 01827 67714
E: info@s-v-c.co.uk
W: www.s-v-c.co.uk

Vehicle Wiring Products Ltd. 9 Buxton Court, Manners Industrial Estate, Ilkeston, Derbyshire DE7 8EF.
T: 0115 9305454
E: sales@vehicleproducts.co.uk
W: www.vehicle-wiring-products.co.uk

West Mercia Mechanical Services, 10 Arrow Road, Telford TF5 0LF.
T: 01952 247007
E: info@autoelectricsupplies.co.uk
W: www.autoelectricsupplies.co.uk

Notes

Notes

Notes

SUBSCRIBE
TODAY AND NEVER MISS AN ISSUE

3 EASY WAYS TO PAY

By Post:

Unit12 Thesiger Close
Worthing
West Sussex
BN11 2RN

By Phone:

01903 236268

Online At:

www.completekitcar.co.uk

August 2009

September 2009

October 2009

November 2009

December 2009

January 2010

February 2010

March 2010

SAVE 15%!

Discounts using the CKC Subs Club Card

FREE KEYRING

...and get a cracking good read!